THE MAN WHO MISTOOK HIMSELF FOR THE MESSIAH

— A MEMOIR —

[signature]

BRYN GENELLE DITMARS

Dear Linda,

Thanks for the support. It's been a pleasure.
Be sure to add up the first letter of each paragraph,
to spell the titles of my 55 other books.

Tellwell Talent
www.tellwell.ca

ISBN
978-1-77302-156-0 (Paperback)
978-1-77302-155-3 (eBook)

TABLE OF CONTENTS

FOREWORD

I WAS NOT MYSELF. WHO BETTER THAN A SOLIPSISTIC SEARCHER FOR meaning to despair with these words? Schizophrenia insidiously, then dramatically, permeated Bryn's ability to discern fact from fiction regarding his identity and purpose in this life. As the dis-order crept in, reality shrank, and the results are detailed in this memoir. "The Man Who Mistook Himself for the Messiah" is the struggle for, and conquest of, sanity's most important quest: To know yourself. As Bryn slipped, repeatedly, into psychosis, that pursuit of self-knowledge was crippled. He believed that he was someone else. He believed he was the Messiah.

As I read over Bryn's draft, I wondered at his use of the lowercase-led "messiah," in lieu of "Messiah." He replied that, in his mind, there was no significant distinction between the two. I, though, pointed out that there have been many "anointed ones," messiahs, while Christianity and Judaism, for example, ascribe to a past (by the former) or coming (by the latter) singular Messiah to "save" them. Bryn then wrote back that he had felt "99% messiah, 1% Messiah." It is burden enough to be convinced that you are one of mankind's saviours (to work alongside the others) but even 1% of the time feeling that you are the One, Only, and All to save the entirety of all who have ever lived is a profession that reeks of tragedy and death. The immense duty of being the Messiah surely has further mad-dened the vulnerable mind of many a schizophrenic.

For while whole-hearted belief that one is the Messiah may be intoler-ably stressful, it is also common, at least among the ranks of the mentally ill. Many a psych ward has held Christs. While I have yet to subscribe to the delusion of religious Saviour, I (who also have been diagnosed with schizophrenia) do believe that my brain can regenerate (after assault from voracious microscopic rats who consume the grey, jelly-like mass of my brain; yes, I am prone to strange delusions). This neuroregeneration would be unprecedented in mankind, and so I strongly felt the need to be "sacrificed" for scientists to probe the underlying biochemistry of this miraculous, life-saving and life-altering condition. In other words, I was the Neuroscientific Messiah. On that level, I can empathize with Bryn. Between us, could we have saved the world both spiritually and corporally?

But no, Bryn is no more a messiah than I. We - friends, family, psychiatry - tell him that, to his great relief. Though, I do confess, I must allow that if there has to be one Messiah among the 108 billion people who have ever lived on this small planet, then Bryn has a one in 108 billion chances of being that Messiah (odds likewise minute but possible of being one of several messiahs). A tiny, remote possibility - but people do win the lottery. As a scientist, I say that the immensely improbable may yet be possible. I hope my statistics offer Bryn solace, not fear. *God only knows*, writes Bryn.

Then there are the statistics of schizophrenia. 1% of the world's population have this brain disorder. Like Bryn, I accept my diagnosis, determined to make lemonade out of the lemons. We both communicate our stories by way of public speaking, peer support, and, now, by our memoirs (his being but a small part of his extensive and impressive body of written work). We see how this impacts others: those living with schizophrenia, their friends and families, and professionals or those in training (such as nursing students). In this, we find and offer hope.

Still, there are the days when we are determined to be cured. Can we cure ourselves? Can mental health professionals cure us? Why do tiny little antipsychotic pills change us so drastically?

There is a growing movement to "free" people of the supposed tyranny of pill-taking for psychosis. *Those medications change your brain!* they say, implying that this is a terrible thing. But, with a MSc in Neuroscience in my back pocket, I say: *Yes, please.* For our brains are forever changing, each moment altering our neuronal biochemistry. If, unmedicated, my brain changes further and further into the substrate of psychosis, then

I desperately would like whatever can instead cause the changes that underlie mental wellness.

Thus and likewise, Bryn is dedicated to taking his regimen of olanzapine and risperidone, two powerful antipsychotics. Despite some side-effects, they have given him his life back. He is able to *be himself.*

But wait. Is Bryn really "Bryn" or is he but who his meds make him? When we live on psychiatric medication, does it take away who we really are? Does it substitute a false self, taking our true identity away? Who are we when we regularly consume those pills?

In his memoir, Bryn repeatedly and emphatically takes a stand on this issue. *I was not myself,* he wrote of when the psychosis gripped him by the throat. He believed things, said things, did things, that did not match who he was either before or after his active mental dis-order. He was suffering. It is the dis-ease that makes us alien, not the meds. Bryn rightly notes that other people close to him, who knew him well, demanded his pharmaceutical treatment not in order to change him, but bring him back. "Is it me or my meds?" is the wrong question. Rather, the proper one is: "Is it me or my psychosis?"

Untreated, or under-treated, schizophrenia caused Bryn to be *not himself. I had been led astray by my illness,* writes Bryn. Medication, with concurrent self-care: nourishment and sleep; activity and productivity; strong relationships with family and friends: it all has led Bryn back to a place where his solipsism is based on the reality of his life. He, I, and "the King of Chronic Insomnia" delight to debate our three journeys of intra- and inter-personal knowledge.

As we live, taking medication and keeping our appointments, we might, as Bryn did, hear the word, "cured." I think it is meant well, as an encouragement or accomplishment, but it left Bryn wondering, as I too might question, *Is this as good as it is going to get?* We are, yes, in a good space, but we ought not be so contained. *All I want... is a cure for my schizophrenia,* laments Bryn. But like an insidious cancer, how do you eradicate every tenacious tentacle and ensure that it will not regrow? We have no promises, and Bryn still has his moments of symptoms. Schizophrenia will likely always be with him - a cure is unforeseen in his lifetime - but he has been given enough sanity to keep him saying, *I am myself.*

July 14, 2016

Erin Emiru (nee Hawkes)
Author, *When Quietness Came: A Neuroscientist's Personal Journey with Schizophrenia.*

"My dad told me that an old man told him
that the lake in the valley is bottomless."

PROLOGUE

FAR AS I'M CONCERNED, IF I GOT A PENNY FOR EVERY HOUR I'VE SPENT
in a psychiatrist's office, I'd be a millionaire by now. This might be a little
bit of an exaggeration. Maybe. Just a little bit. But, I remind myself of
the evident fact that now, on December 12th, 2015, at the age of 36, as I
write this, I have less than seventy-two bucks to my name. Besides which,
here in Canada, pennies don't even exist. So, apparently, that solves
that problem.

Aside from my meagre financial status, I'm living a very happy and
fulfilling life. And, my brother, aged 34, forever offers the reminder that
the purpose of life is to be happy. Enough said.

The truth of the matter is that I have spent the last 13 years, navigating
the mental health care system. From breakdown, to crisis situation, to
diagnosis, to treatment, and from relapse to relapse, and finally to something resembling recovery. However, the term 'recovery' is a tricky one.
My colleagues and I agree that, on the path to mental wellness, with all
of its ups and downs, it's not so much a matter of desperately attempting
to regain our previous stability, as it is a process of re-'dis'-covery. We, as
human beings, are all enlisted in the school of self-knowledge, some of
us more astute than others. I am constantly rediscovering my self, the
essence of which can and will be found by way of revealing my own
true nature.

Has it really been that long since I was diagnosed, back in May of 2002? Has it really been 13 years? Well, yes, actually. My son was born in July of 2002. And, he is now 13. He's already almost as tall as me, and his shoes are one size bigger than mine. Whenever I look at him, I am reminded of just how far I've come on my road to 'recovery'.

Every day that passes, I consider myself to be very fortunate. Fortunate to be loved, and fortunate to be alive. Now, provided I don't explode with an overwhelming sense of sincere gratitude, and as long as I stay focused on my life purpose, and with a certain amount of goodwill, I will live to a ripe old age, old enough to see my son become a father. I have always maintained that it's a matter of work and luck. Persistence for the work, and patience for the luck.

Really, as I look back into the past and reflect upon my life, the verity of my philosophy is only reinforced. But, I cannot, in all my power, accurately ascertain what the future holds. There is only the present moment. And, keep in mind that, if hindsight is 20/20 vision, self-prophetic foresight is as blind as an injured barn-bat. All I know is that, for these past few years, I have been waking up in the morning, looking forward to what the day has to hold. If that is not an indication of true happiness, I don't know what is.

Shall I glance ever backwards and retrace my steps, the steps that have led me here, the experiences that have brought me to this point? Yes! The details, many heinous and many joyous and many triumphant and many courageous, the details of my life's events give a voice to the voiceless, and very possibly they will give insights into the many manifestations of this disease from which I suffer. Schizophrenia is a brain disease. When a person breaks his leg, pain signals make their way to his brain, and he quickly realizes that he has broken his leg. So, he goes to the hospital and gets an x-ray, and the doctor bandages his leg in a cast, and recovery is 100% probable. But, when the brain is what's broken, the propensity to address the problem is often impaired, because the problem itself is not properly identified. The individual's lack of insight is called 'anosognosia'. Many people with broken brains never realize they have a mental illness. In fact, that inability to realize they're ill is actually a symptom in and of itself. I'm one of the lucky ones. I have gained insight, enough insight so that my illness is manageable.

Ordained by God? Maybe. Gifted? Perhaps. But, what is for certain is that I live a life, however happy and fulfilling, in which I am required to take medication… And, every day, I take my medication. And, I do so religiously. I owe it to myself. I owe it to all those around me. Mainstream pharmaceutical anti-psychotic medication. Every single night before I go to sleep. And, let me tell you, I sleep *like a log*.

Now, I remember back to a time in my life that proved to be pivotal. I was a patient at the forensic psychiatric hospital. Everyone on the ward was on medication. And, everyone on the ward paced. Back and forth, up and down the long sterile hallway, we would pace, walking cool and calculated steps, shuffling this way and that. After six months of incarceration there, I had adopted the behaviour. And, even today, 10 years later, I often find myself pacing the floor of my apartment. And, even today, I remember those other patients on that ward. I'm in mental health housing, and the apartments in my building are somewhat small, so it necessitates me to basically walk in circles. Either in circles or simply back and forth. But, I am wholly convinced that, after more than a year of living here, I've walked the equivalent of several hundred marathons. And, if only all my cool and calculated steps had been in the same direction, I would have ended up in Halifax by now. I suppose this is also another slight exaggeration. Maybe. Just a little bit.

CATHEDRAL BELLS

CHAPTER 1

YEAH, CHRISTMAS IS FAST APPROACHING, AND THE NEW YEAR IS JUST around the corner. This year has been a good one. It has proven to be the total fruition of all the work and luck that went into this past decade. I walked some really dark paths in these past years. My son, Gabriel, remains the light of my life, and I am left to contemplate my experiences of fatherhood.

Now, in the great night of time, as dark are all the days, the winter solstice reminds us all that light will slowly return. My new year's resolution is to get out of debt and to stay out of debt. Credit cards are useful. And, in emergencies, they can come in handy. I only owe less than four hundred dollars. But, keep in mind that the average Canadian citizen is upwards of twenty-six thousand dollars in debt. By the time that my peer support work payment cheque comes through at the end of this month, I might be well on my way to freedom.

My occupation is a funny one. I'm a peer support worker. Have been for the past three years. A peer support worker is a person with lived experience of a mental illness who has gone through the training program offered by Vancouver Coastal Health, and works in the community in order to better the lives of others who are living with a mental health diagnosis. I currently have two contracts with two mental health teams, with a total of five clients, whom I see every week. Together, we establish the goals, and I help my clients reach those goals, often with baby-steps, and sometimes with leaps and bounds.

Except, meanwhile, I have to maintain *my* mental health. I receive treatment myself. I try my best to manage my symptoms myself. And, I have a variety of struggles of my own. I know that the work I do helps to improve the quality of life of my clients, but it doesn't end there. It is also therapeutic for me, as well. In fact, I even believe that it has kept me out of hospital. It gets me out of my own head, and it gives me an opportunity to contribute to the community. There was once a time when I myself could have used a peer support worker. Now, I'm giving back.

Don't get me wrong. I'm still receiving care from a psychiatrist. But, he insists that what remains of my schizophrenia is only 'residual'. My affect is not blunted in any way whatsoever. I am responding well to treatment. My lifestyle is healthy. I have my priorities straight. And, my behaviour doesn't lack spontaneity. At my most recent psychiatrist appointment, he said that I was 'cured'. I think that what he meant by that was that my condition is as good as it's gonna get. With medication, that is.

Yeah, Christmas is coming soon. And, I am doing fine. Now, imagine celebrating Christmas, while identifying *as* Christ. I have been there. I have done that. Several times in fact. Let me tell you, it is not fun. In my present state of mind, I know intellectually that I am not the Messiah, but I still perceive things that indicate that to me. There are seven billion people on this planet, seventy million of whom are schizophrenic, and only one messiah. Talk about small chances!

Actually, I'm relieved that I am not the messiah. It's one thing to have to take pills for the rest of my life. It's another thing entirely to have to save the world. I'll take my pills, thank you very much. Apparently, there's a mental hospital in Jerusalem, in which all the patients believe that they are the messiah. At meal times, the conversations must be positively hilarious. The arguments must be rather ridiculous, indeed. But, the suffering involved in these delusions is no laughing matter. The messianic complex that I've had for most of my life can be simply defined and summarized with one word. 'Tragic'. However, it's important to have a healthy sense of humour.

Reflecting on one of my more recent experiences, I can honestly thank my involvement with peer support work for the fact that I met two of my best friends. I met The King Of Chronic Insomnia back in 2011, when we attended the same peer support work training program. He and I have since then shared a million coffees, and we dream up dreams together, in the form of fascinating intellectual and philosophical conversations, every word of which I savour. I met The Quiet One, back in May of 2014, when she attended one of my talks at the Vancity Theatre. She was born the same month and the same year as me, and has a similar diagnosis. In fact, The King Of Chronic Insomnia, The Quiet One, and I all have the same brain disease. It's known as paranoid schizophrenia. But, the three of us are very different from one another.

Each one of us is entirely unique. We meet weekly, to debrief over coffee. We support each other, seeing as all three of us are peer support workers. My son, Gabriel, came along with me one week earlier this year. He understands it perfectly, as 'peer support support… support for the peer support'.

So, anyway, back in September, I went to Victoria with The King Of Chronic Insomnia and The Quiet One. We met at Broadway and Cambie, one fine summer morning, and took the bus to Tsawwassen ferry terminal, where we then caught the boat to Swartz Bay. Finally, on Vancouver Island, we rode the double-decker bus in to the downtown area of B.C.'s capital city. Our plan was to visit Russell Books, which just so happens to be the best bookstore in the world, shop around, stay the night, shop around the next day, and then go home with precious literary treasures in our satchels.

Yeah, so, the three high-functioning schizophrenic bibliophiles went wild in the bookstore on the first day. Then, The King Of Chronic Insomnia and I checked in to a hostel for the night, being sure to watch out for any sign of bed bugs. The Quiet One stayed with her family, who lived a half hour walk away. The hostel room, which we had reserved, was very small, just enough room for a bunk bed. I searched for a plug outlet, and was sure to plug in my e-cig vaporizer battery before I went to sleep. I took the top bunk. The King Of Chronic Insomnia took the bottom bunk. And, as I drifted off to dream-land, I could hear him down below, turning the pages of a paperback novel. The lamplight didn't bother me. He and I are like brothers.

Did I dream? Probably. Did I remember my dreams? No, not at all. I woke up at sunrise, only to find my friend, still very deeply asleep. I looked out the window. It was yet another beautiful sunny day. After about an hour of sitting there, watching my friend sleep, I woke him up. He jolted suddenly out of bed, and he got dressed, while I went to the bathroom down the hall. We munched on a few chocolate covered almonds, and went downstairs. After checking out of the hostel, we walked outside, not knowing exactly how to pass the time before the bookstore opened. But, the world was our oyster, and we were happy to be alive in it, like a couple of oddly shaped pearls.

Until 10:00am, we wandered the lonely streets, a pair of bohemian pilgrims inspired by life. We found the nearest Starbucks, and feasted on croissants and coffee. I texted The Quiet One, who suggested that the three of us meet at the bookstore soon. The King Of Chronic Insomnia and I did our best to pass the time. I took pictures on my cell phone, and puffed on my vaporizer. It was a glorious day, but there was no one else to be seen there. Just the two of us, and a bunch of buses, and a stream of anonymous taxis.

And, in the distance, coming from the church down the road, we could hear the cathedral bells. It occurred to us that it was Sunday. Our only prayer was that the bookstore, once it opened, had a bathroom. He and I were the first ones through that door, eager to find gems on the shelves that lined the walls. The Quite One showed up soon after, when I luckily discovered an entire section dedicated to books by Gibran. And, to add to my existing collection, I purchased another copy of 'The Prophet' for $5.99. It was a score.

Later on, returning to Swartz Bay on another double decker bus, taking the ferry to Tsawwassen, then catching a bus, then transferring to a skytrain, we finally arrived back at City Hall Station, at Broadway and Cambie. It was after sunset. And, the sky was clear and starry. Also, the moon was full and round, eclipsing before our very eyes. Puffing on a cigarette (seeing as my vaporizer had broken and ran out of charge), I walked with The Quiet One westward. I arrived home around 9:00pm. Home to my collection of manuscripts. Home to my coffee maker. Home to where I belonged in mental health housing. Home, with a song in my heart.

A POCKET FULL OF GOLD
CHAPTER 2

SO, MY LIFE BEGAN AT 5:11AM, WAY BACK ON THE MORNING OF FEBRUARY 23rd of the year 1979, when, as fate would have it, I was born. Apparently, according to popular statistics, babies born in and around the late winter months have an increased chance of developing schizophrenia. We don't know why that is. But, my guess is that it has something to do with not getting enough vitamin D by way of sunlight, or the coldness causing added stress to the mother's body, or common winter viral infection. Maybe I'm wrong, but this is a theory.

Like many human beings, I don't quite know for sure what really happened in the world before I was born, nor do I know for sure that there was a 'world' at all. There was the first world war, the second world war, as well as the iconic 60's generation. But, sometimes I wonder if all of world history is merely a convenient contextual fabrication designed to position the human race strategically in a particular time and place, all in order to add importance to our existence. This belief is actually a big part of my delusions. As I struggle with it on a daily basis, my mind constantly affirms this idea, and always comes back to the universal truth that we are all but particles of stardust, floating somewhere in an ocean of galaxies in a vast and virtually infinite cosmos. Whether true or false, it is truly humbling in that it reminds me of my relative insignificance.

Evidently, I emerged into this incarnation in the same way a king sits upon a throne. My soul has found its chair of rest, for the remainder of this life anyway. I was the firstborn son of a carpenter and a midwife. My dad remembers me winking from out of the womb, two weeks late, and blessed with an unmistakable sense of mortal awareness. The sun had not yet fully risen, and the spring had not yet sprung. Both diurnally and seasonally, darkness was making its divine descent, retreating to give way to light's prodigious return.

Emerging head-first, with a small brown mole on my right cheek, I accepted this world, and this world accepted me. My mother had been in labour all night long. There, upon the bloodstained blankets of the bed, at home in our house on Granite Road, in a residential area of Nelson, B.C., I was received by the sure hands of a midwife, at the base of Kootenay Valley, between the ominous mountain walls of forested land.

Pretty soon, I crawled. And, pretty soon, I walked and talked. There is a story of my father getting a vasectomy around this time. However, the procedure was quickly proven to be unsuccessful when, shortly after, my brother was born. Rumour has it that the doctor who performed the operation was indeed Roman Catholic. None the less, at the age of two-and-a-half years, I was blessed with a newborn sibling. Reuben and I have the same mother and father, and primarily the same genetics, but he has not grown up to develop schizophrenia. Over the years, he has been a big source of love and support, often being the only person whom I trust during times of acute psychosis. All I can say, is thank God for Catholicism!

Now, Reuben and I were also blessed with three half-sisters. Our father had two daughters before we were born. And, our mother had one daughter before we were born. He and I are Kootenay boys at heart. I remember playing with him in the forest, during endless summer days, where we lived in Wild Horse Creek, a self-proclaimed 'hippie-commune', catching frogs and garter snakes, swimming in the pond, eating wild rhubarb and wild strawberries, happy and healthy young kids, with our whole lives ahead of us. We would spend all day playing in the forest, dancing down old dirt roads, and then returning to our old wooden house at sunset, where wooden posts and beams reflected a warm golden light from the flames of kerosene lanterns.

And, Reuben and I had friends to play with. However, I think it's safe to say that I had more friends than he did, seeing as many of mine were imaginary. You see, I frequented one particular tree in a secret place in our front yard, where I believed fairies and gnomes and elves lived. I was sure of it. Under the lowest branches of that pine tree, where the trunk met the soil, I was absolutely certain that imaginary creatures dwelt. So, throughout the course of my day, I would collect things. Feathers, rocks, pebbles, and bits of colourful broken glass gradually found their way into the pockets of my pants, and I would place them all beneath that one tree, as offerings to the dwellers of a mythical elfin kingdom.

Kissed once by birth, and kissed once more by life, I was blessed with a fertile imagination, at that tender young age of five. Little did anyone know that twenty years later I would be, by that very same imagination, cursed. Anyway, whatever the exact nature of my histrionic personality, I was experiencing hallucinations, for lack of a better term. One day, I was staring into space (which I remember doing often in those days), with my knees on the seat of our big red couch, leaning my belly heavily against the back, gazing dazedly down behind the furniture, to where the floor joined to the wooden log walls. And, suddenly, I saw a small old man no more that eighteen inches tall. He was a wizard, as ever there was one, with a long white beard, dressed in a navy blue robe decked with designs of moon and star, and a tall pointed hat with a big black brim.

Eternally, I gazed, awestruck by my vision. Then, the wizard looked up at me. He was frightened by what he saw, waved his wooden staff, and magically disappeared from sight. That was my first visual hallucination, but it surely was not my last.

Dark was the womb from whence I had come. And, brilliant the world into which I had arrived, filled with beauty, truth, and the all-powerful ability to dream dreams. I remember dreaming of wealth, when my brother and I were first introduced to the concept of money by our father. As a form of allowance, he gave us a one dollar bill. It was old and worn and creased and withered. I, being the 'big' brother, thought of all the possible ways to make use of it. I could have saved it, shared it with my brother, or taken it all and spent it on candy. But, ever the fair child, I told my brother that he could have half of it. I told him that I would tear it in half, and he could then choose which half he wanted. The idea was that the bigger the half, the bigger would be the value. When our mom and dad saw what we had done, they laughed and explained how money doesn't work that way. So, they tried to salvage the bill, by rejoining both halves with two pieces of clear scotch tape.

CATERPILLARS AND WOULD-BE BUTTERFLIES

CHAPTER 3

THE PROFUNDITY OF CHILDISH LOGIC! AH, YES. ANOTHER EXAMPLE OF this occurred right around the time when my big sister (on my mother's side) gave me something that she held very dear to her heart. A small grey jewelry box. It had hinges, and kind of unfolded as it opened, revealing a small shelf of sorts. She had used it to store her bracelets, earrings, and necklaces in. But, I had other plans for its use.

With it empty, save for a glittery round sticker of a unicorn which wouldn't come off the lid, I dreamed of all the things I could do with it. Give it to the fairies and elves. Keep food in it to snack on. Or, I thought of something else. Something more magical. You see, I had recently been introduced to the concept of chrysalis.

Except, with my childish imagination, I thought I could 'play God' so to speak. It was the middle of summer, and there were many things going on in the natural world. There were fuzzy orange caterpillars and gorgeous monarch butterflies, as well as everything in between. Cocoons. Dense white cobwebs in the branches of the cottonwood trees. I had put two and two together, and come up with an idea.

Not knowing what miracles were going to happen, I collected three caterpillars, and put them in my jewelry box. Watching them crawl around the bottom of the box, I suddenly realized that they were probably hungry. So, I put a small green leaf of lettuce in with them. And, proud of myself for thinking of it, before I closed the box for the night, I took a black felt pen and drew my best rendition of a butterfly on the underside of the lid. The caterpillars would eat the lettuce, the lettuce would help them grow strong, they would look up at the emblem, and by morning they would emerge as butterflies!

This did not go as planned. I woke up in the morning, running over to the jewelry box. And, opening the box, instead of finding butterflies, I found three dead caterpillars. I was devastated. It was my first brush with mortality.

Yeah, we can imitate the world, and we can even play God. But, when we mess around with nature, we realize our mistake.

Then, for some reason, on New Year's Eve, my father was taking care of me and my brother. It was cold and dark and snowy there in Wild Horse Creek. We went down the road to our neighbours who had a big sled run going down from their porch. Before midnight, and before the party really got started, I went down the steep slope on a big black inner tube, and took a deadly turn on the jump. I fell on my shoulder and broke my collar bone.

While I was crying and sobbing and yelling and screaming, my brother peed his pants. Our father took us home. The next day, the three of us went into Nelson hospital. X-Rays proved my collar bone was broken. So, the doctor told me I needed to wear a sling. I told him that I would wear the sling if he gave me a can of orange crush from the vending machine. He agreed. I took the pop and drank it, then hid under a nearby table. I did not wear the sling. And, my shoulder healed all by itself.

Enough about my childhood angst. I simply wish to convey how I saw the world as a kid. Also around this time, I was in kindergarten at the Waldorf school. I used to swallow my chewing gum. And, while playing in the sandbox, I discovered eating sand. And, the smell of beeswax crayons is prominent in my memory. I noticed that some of my friends had a habit of sucking their thumbs. I remember trying to suck my thumb just to see what all the fuss was about. Five minutes before, however, I had spilled some orange juice on my hand. So, when I sucked on my thumb, it tasted like orange juice. I deduced that this was why my friends insisted on doing so.

Like the other kids my age, I was learning a lot. My big sister (on my mother's side) taught me how to tie my shoes. To me, it was like the holy grail of things to know. I watched her loop the laces, and tie the knots. It took me a while to master it. But, eventually I did.

Vast were the realms of knowledge that I had yet to gain. And, many were the things I taught my brother. Half of a dollar bill is not worth fifty cents. Caterpillars die in boxes. Thumbs don't always taste like orange juice. Eating sand makes you gag. And, last but not least, doctors can and will be manipulated.

Each and every day that passed, however, I saw my parents growing further and further apart. My mother went to Vancouver, to further her education and establish her career in the reemerging profession of midwifery leaving me and my brother in the care of our father. He hired a nanny of sorts, a french Canadian woman. She had a son who was about my age. She made us our meals, and taught us to say 'finis' once we had eaten everything on our plates. Recently, I have come to use that same term at the very bottom of the last page of every book I've written. Some things are never unlearned.

THE VOICE OF GOD
CHAPTER 4

THERE ARE MANY STORIES OF MYSTICAL RELIGIOUS FIGURES WHO report hearing the voice of God as children. I'm not a mystic. But, as early as age five, I have heard voices. The earliest memory I have of hearing someone speak when no one was there, it is very clear in my recollection. The voice came to me when I was with my father.

He was holding my hand, as the two of us were walking down the street, in Nelson, my home town. We were coming from a dentist appointment, on our way to get a milkshake. That was when I heard a voice of an old man.

Except, it wasn't the voice of my father. I could tell, because his lips weren't moving. The voice (of God?) spoke clearly, telling me that I was going to die at the age of thirty-three, and that my soulmate's name was Sarah. And, to show just how insidious the psychotic hallucinations of paranoid schizophrenia can be, I should mention that I was afraid of my own death until I turned thirty-four. Also, I have had seven girlfriends in my life, and three of them were named Sarah. Let's just say that my thirty-fourth birthday was a cause for celebration, and I still think back to the voice every time I meet someone named Sarah.

Concurrently, around this time, my parents were breaking up. I was about five, and my brother was two and a half. Our dad and his wife, Jen, rented a small house in Strathcona on the east side of Vancouver. And, our mom was staying with friends on the west side of Vancouver. Reuben and I would spend time at both houses regularly.

And, that's when I became friends with Gabriel's Godfather. He was a few months younger than me, and I was amazed by his extensive lego collection, his coin collection, and of course the fact that he could play the piano. He had a computer, on which he and my brother and I would play a game called 'King's Quest'.

Really, now as I look back on this time of my life, I am grateful. Grateful for the fact that my parents were making an effort to get along, and grateful for the fact that my father had an artist for a companion. Jen showed me and my brother all about drawing, painting, and we spent endless hours making crafts together. She inspired me to become the artist I am today.

Perfectly unaware of my hallucinations and delusions, as well as my wild imagination, my friends and family were happy with how my brother and I were turning out. Reuben and I started elementary school at Emily Carr, on the corner of Oak street and King Edward. I was in grade one, and he was in preschool. Our mother's place was only two blocks away from the school, where she was sharing a house with a single mother and her two sons. The youngest of the two boys was my age, and the older one was almost twelve.

Enlightened by the fact that mom and dad were collaborating with their parental responsibilities, I was nurtured in my growth. But, my big imagination was not merely a phase. It stayed with me, day in and day out. You see, the single mother we lived with had a beautiful old wooden loom used for weaving tapestries and such. On the loom, there was a small glass prism hanging from a thread. I referred to it, on more than one occasion, not as a 'loom' but as a 'prism holder'.

Now, at the age of six or seven, I was doing very well at school, even though the first day of grade one had brought me close to tears, and I was liked by all my classmates. I recall a certain Valentine's Day, when we were supposed to exchange cards. My mother bought a big book of cards. My brother took half, and I took half. That left each of us with about twenty cards. I signed all twenty of them to this one particular girl in my class. On the back of every card, I wrote: 'To Vivian, Love Bryn'. However, when February 14th rolled around, I didn't have the courage or the conviction to put them all in her cubby-hole. That year, none of my friends got cards from me.

There was Ms. Burton for grade one, and Mrs. Crocket for grades two and three. Then, in grade four, my teacher was Ms. Walker. She was a nice old lady. When it came to dealing with my precociousness, she was definitely up for the task.

Ensuing my tenth birthday, I developed a severe phobia of food. I thought it was a form of poison, toxic to my body. I had recently gotten sick at a friend's party, and was put off of not just junk food but all food. I also thought that all the world's problems were my fault. I would spend hours in my bed, crying. There was also a bit of hypochondria involved. I was afraid that I was sick and I was worried that my brother would get sick as well.

Reclined on the living room couch, with pillows and blankets, I refused to eat or drink anything. I remember my poor mom, sitting beside me, begging me to eat or drink. Soon, she resorted to using a small syringe with which she tried desperately to put a thimbleful of apple juice into my small dry mouth. I resisted. I was reading the Narnia series by C.S. Lewis, having out of body experiences, and was preoccupied with a delusional belief that I had lived this same life seven times before. The deja vu lasted for about six weeks. As well, I experienced a strange recurring feeling every time I would close my eyes, a feeling of being huge beyond belief then completely tiny and insignificant.

Such it was that my anorexia progressed and worsened, to the point where I was admitted to Children's Hospital. They put me in a bed on the cancer ward. On intravenous, I lay there, surrounded by dying children who were either bald or balding from the heavy chemotherapy that was being administered to them. After each meal, they would vomit into a bedpan. Now, I was certain I was ill. Why else would I have been in a room full of dying children? My logic was impenetrable.

And, finally, when I had lost a lot of weight, skin and bones because I refused to eat or drink, a doctor came into my room, and told me that I was going to die if I went on like this. I cried and cried, with my mother by my side. I was complaining of nausea, and assured her that I would get sick to my stomach if I ate anything.

Poor mom. During my stay at the hospital, she had come to my room daily, with bags full of all the food she knew I liked. Anyway, a miracle happened. I agreed to eat, as proof that I wasn't trying to starve myself to death. She handed me a small container of blueberry yogurt. I struggled, putting two spoonfuls of yogurt into my mouth, and swallowing. But, after two bites, I was full. My stomach must have shrunk to the size of a walnut, as a result of my anorexia.

Praise to my mother. She was so happy. Ecstatic, really. And, I was proud of myself as well. Breakfast came to my bed the very next morning, and I ate half of a piece of toast. Then, a couple days later, I had my first bowel movement in weeks. And, so it went.

Returning to school, though still pale and anxious, I was welcomed back to the grade four classroom, where Ms. Walker was happy to see me again. Then, when Easter arrived, she handed out chocolate eggs to all the students. I was the only ten year old in that room who declined the offer. Commenting on the strange peculiarity, she called me a purist. Actually, that terminology was entirely accurate. Because, from then on in until a few years later, I obsessively read the ingredients of the food I ate, staying far away from anything that had sugar in it. I now know that sugar is essential to the human diet, but at the time it stood for the devil in my mind.

Eventually, I graduated from elementary school, the valedictorian of my class, with nothing but straight A's, and received the award for best all-round student. I was also very involved in baseball, soccer, and cross-country running. There was nothing 'wrong' with me, and on the outside I was completely functional. In fact, I was excelling in everything I was doing.

No need for a mental health diagnosis, I continued living my life in a way that was in fact quite enlightened. Art therapy had helped me immensely. After about a dozen sessions, my therapist suggested that my mother buy me a journal and a pen, insisting that writing would be good for me, as a way to get my thoughts down on paper.

The voice of God.

I remember just how loud my thoughts were. In the back of my mind, I imagined a sort of running commentary that seemed to go on and on internally. But, there were no more auditory hallucinations. I began to feel very clear about my life purpose, having come 'close to death' as my doctor had put it so bluntly, years previous. I had come close to the same fate that those caterpillars had, in my jewelry box, back at Wild Horse Creek. Evidently, the lid of the jewelry box, in which I was held captive, had opened just in time. Blossoming as a bright young thirteen year old boy, I was becoming less of a worm and more of a butterfly.

Chrysalis was upon me. Dad and Jen had purchased an old heritage house in Strathcona, down the street from where they had been previously renting. That summer, I was in the living room, when the telephone rang. It was my soccer coach, informing me that I was chosen to be part of the Vancouver under fifteen metro soccer team, and we were heading off together on a trip to Europe, to play in an international tournament.

Eternities of trial, turbulence, and turmoil were dissolving from off my back, like coils of dead skin. I was excited. No longer hearing the voice of a God in whom I didn't even believe, I was doing what kids should do, and began playing soccer as the team's right midfielder. We took the airplane to Amsterdam, where we were assigned a private tour bus, traveling through Holland, Belgium, and Germany, playing two games a day for fourteen days. My teammates elected me to speak into the microphone at opening ceremonies, and we proceeded to have the time of our lives. We stayed in four-star hotels, and toured the countryside. We won half the games and lost the other half of the games. India came in first place, when the tournament concluded. Then, it was back to Vancouver to begin high school. High school, with an emphasis on 'high'.

CHRISTMAS EVE
CHAPTER 5

MY CURRENT PREDICAMENT IS A PECULIAR ONE. IT BECOMES APPARENT to me every time I walk into my kitchen. You see, positioned on the corner of one of the shelves, there is a small tupperware container, in which there is another container, in which there are six small gel capsules of pure CBD oil. CBD stands for Cannabidiol, an ingredient in the marijuana plant. But, unlike THC, which is the ingredient that causes mild psychosis, CBD is the counter-balance, which is the anti-psychotic ingredient.

In countries such as Sweden, CBD is prescribed to treat schizophrenia. I've never been to Sweden, but sometimes I wish I lived there. Because, CBD has no known side-effects. The medication I am currently taking is known to cause diabetes, among other unpleasant things. I'm sure that Canada will eventually catch on to using CBD to treat psychotic illnesses. But, I'm not sure I can wait that long. The question is, do I *have* to wait that long?

Donated to me recently by a friend of one of my ex-girlfriends, those ominous capsules of pure CBD are forever tempting me to go against the grain of modern psychiatry. My intuition is telling me that CBD would be helpful. But, it's been sitting patiently on my kitchen shelf for two weeks now, and I haven't had the courage to try it.

Now, it's Christmas Eve, and I still haven't tried it. I've come to the sober conclusion that I should not risk it. I insist that, if and when I try CBD, I would demand that my doctor agree to see me through the process of the therapy. Apparently, in Vancouver these days, there are medicinal marijuana dispensaries popping up on every street corner, walking that fine line between the legal and the illegal. And, I am an open-minded kinda guy, but I am wary of experimental medicine.

I saw a documentary about this girl named Charlotte, who had epilepsy. She would have epileptic seizures about three hundred times a week. And, every single one of those seizures was potentially fatal. Then, when her parents gave her CBD, she was having only one seizure a day. The brothers in Colorado who grew the strain were amazed to see the parents requesting it. Normally, most people buy only the strains that are high in THC. They were going to just throw the crop of the CBD strain in the garbage. But, when they saw how healing it was for little Charlotte, they called it 'Charlotte's Web'.

Good for them! And, good for Charlotte's parents too.

Her mother and father moved to Colorado, where it is legal, all in order to save her life. I don't have epilepsy, but I do have an illness that was brought on by my use of THC in my teenage years and my early twenties. My schizophrenia became severe, right around the time I smoked an entire plant in two months in the fall of 2001.

Then again, my brother also did drugs as a teenager, and he did not develop schizophrenia. So, I guess I just have to have patience, until someday down the road Canada legalizes and regulates the production, distribution and use of both recreational and medicinal marijuana. My psychiatrist has been practicing for nearly five decades, and has advised me time and time again to stay well away from any and every form of the drug.

Voices and visions of things that are not really there have plagued me for sometime now. But, it's Christmas Eve, and I should be thankful. My son is in the Nicola Valley, where there is snow. He is probably having snowball fights with his cousins and the other members of his mother's family. He's with horses and dogs and cats, and probably building snowmen in the fields. Meanwhile, I'm in my apartment in rainy Vancouver, reflecting on my life.

In the world outside my window, the sky is dark. My mother is having Christmas dinner with her daughter's family out in Port Coquitlam. I was invited, but chose not to go. I wish my sister and my niece all the very best.

So, I have a small 'tree' this year, bought for me by my mother, bless her soul. There are a few wrapped presents under it. It's rather awkward, celebrating the birth of the saviour, while struggling to maintain a messianic complex, I must admit. But, I'm doing my best.

If Christ is, perhaps, the bridge between God and Man, I do believe in Him. I'm not a Christian, but I believe in spiritually inspired prophecy. And, Christmastime is so contagious that it is a struggle to resist celebrating with lights and candles and decorations and trees and endless egg nog.

On an hour earlier this afternoon, The King Of Chronic Insomnia came over to my place for coffee. He and I talked about philosophy and religion and spirituality. He gave me two coffee mugs. One for him, and one for me. We'll use them every time he comes to visit me.

Now, I am wishing all the very best of light and warmth and cheer to everyone in my life. I've been a pretty good boy this year, and I don't expect a lump of coal in my stocking. My only concern is that I don't have a chimney. I'll go to sleep tonight, hoping and praying that Santa Claus knows my buzzer number.

Santa, all I want for Christmas this year is a cure for my schizophrenia.

COUNTERCLOCKWISE
CHAPTER 6

MY HIGH SCHOOL CAREER BEGAN PRETTY MUCH RIGHT AFTER MY soccer team returned from Europe. I had been accepted into a program at Ideal Mini School. There were only about a hundred students, twenty students in each of the five grades. It was actually smaller than my elementary school had been, so the only adjustment I had to make was in the downsizing. That, and I had to get used to calling my teachers by their first names.

A small building, pretty much one long hallway to navigate, the alternative school was cozily situated on the corner of 59th and Laurel, down the street from the monstrous mainstream Churchill Secondary School. The first week of grade eight was absolutely delightful, as all the students designed, decorated, and painted the lockers they were assigned. I painted a huge eyeball on my locker, and never found the need for a lock.

Now, it should be known that the students at Ideal were an odd bunch. We were either geniuses or lunatics. Half the student body was gifted, and the other half was troubled. I fit into the 'gifted' category, seeing as I had received straight A's throughout elementary school. Starting out, wearing jeans, a tee-shirt, and running shoes, I was the shortest kid in the school. But, looking around at my fellow classmates, who wore twenty-hole-Doc Martins, ripped camouflage shorts, long-johns, bras over-top of torn sweaters, exotic body-piercings, shaved heads or dyed hair, I felt the need to change my system of self-expression. The next day, and for the rest of my high school career, I came to school dressed as a clown, for lack of a better word, with big balloon yellow pinstripe shorts, giant red suspenders, old army-surplus boots, black and white checkered shirts, and various other grunge-gothic styles. Yes, it definitely qualified as an 'abrupt and sudden change in personality', to paraphrase a popular definition of warning signs of early schizophrenia.

I remember leaving my dad's house in the morning on the way to school, rebelliously slipping on one of Jen's overcoats. I also borrowed her long dangly earrings to wear, on more than one occasion. One memory I have is preparing for the 'Miss Ideal Beauty Contest', where girls (and boys) dressed up as supermodels, competing for prizes based on feminine elegance. I won the award for 'best butt'.

From then on in, all my friends were predicting that I would grow up to be gay. But, so far, that prophecy hasn't materialized. The other thing about Ideal was that there was a smoking section by the trees at the far corner of the school property, where the smokers would go to smoke both cigarettes and joints. All day long, rain or shine, there were students from all five grades, out there across the field, smoking on the hillside. We used to call that part of the schoolyard 'suicide hill'.

Eventually, I became very popular, among both the geniuses and the lunatics alike. The teachers were some of the most inspiring people I'd ever met. There was Phil the math teacher, Rita the art teacher, Monique the French teacher, Aaron the science teacher, Larry the social studies teacher, Georgie the English teacher, and all of them coached us both individually and collectively to be the future cultured young adults we were so destined to become.

So, life was good, and soon I had my first girlfriend. She was a beauty. In fact, in grade eight and grade nine, I had a lot of girlfriends, each of whom was beautiful. We would have sleepover parties, drinking parties, pot-smoking parties, and kissing-game parties. There was this one time when one of my grade nine classmates somehow got the keys to an old Ukrainian church, and invited ten or so of us to spend the night drinking, passing out, and sleeping in the huge religious auditorium, late one Saturday night. We played truth-or-dare.

The straight A's kept on coming. And, I enjoyed my experience at the mini school immensely. I still continued playing baseball and soccer. But, Ideal didn't have a cross-country team, so I omitted that physical activity from my repertoire of athletic endeavours. Nothing was lost, however. In fact, I had my whole life ahead of me. Soon, late in grade nine, I heard from one of the grade twelve students about an outdoors education program that she had attended two years previous. The Trek program was offered to a select group of grade ten students at Prince of Wales Secondary School. It was designed so that the students spent half the year doing intensive amounts of academic work, and then spend the other half of the year building igloos, rock climbing, hiking, kayaking, canoeing, skiing, snowboarding, and many other wilderness adventures. *And,* Prince of Wales had a cross-country team!

Akin to my love of the outdoors, my brother and father both indulged in similar experiential pleasures. Dad and Jen sold their house in Strathcona, and bought a sixty-five acre ranch in the West Chilcotin way up north. Reuben and I spent the summer wandering through the ever-green forest, fishing in the lake, and climbing mountains. The name of the body of fresh water was Rainbow Lake, a term which we casually used in referring to the ranch itself. Midlife crisis? Maybe. The dreaming of a dream? Perhaps. Regardless, our father and his wife made the evident decision to go against the grain of popular modern lifestyle, and bought horses, in a secluded location in central B.C., where there was no running water and no electricity. Just drinking from the creek, baking bread in a wood stove oven, and using a wooden board outhouse.

Then, when I started school in the Trek program, my half of the class were the lucky ones. Lucky, in that we got to do all the academic work first, get the boring stuff out of the way, and then spend the rest of the year doing 'fun' stuff. Right around this time, my brother and I woke up on Christmas morning, only to go into our mother's living room and find two snowboards, boots, and bindings underneath the tree. We were thrilled.

I was doing a lot of babysitting back then, and was able to contribute in my small way to affording my additional wealth and well-being.

Mom was living in a subsidized building reserved for single parents, the disabled, and families with low incomes, and she enrolled in the UBC Nursing School full time for four years. Dad did what he could to help. Meanwhile, my brother and I began experimenting with tobacco, alcohol, LSD, magic mushrooms, and the ever-mysterious marijuana.

Oddly enough, I stayed away from all this, for the most part, while my younger brother proceeded to do the brunt of it. He was going to Kitsilano Secondary down the street, and was struggling in school, hanging out with his rebellious teenage friends, smoking pot, and drinking slurpees spiked with Vodka.

Now, that was the time in my life when I started smoking pot, and that was also the time in my life when I started writing creatively. Grade ten at Prince of Wales, though also a time of healthy pleasure, was often a time of severe existential angst for me. I was the only kid in Trek with a bright green mohawk hairdo, and the only boy who insisted on wearing lengthy silver earrings. But, my marks stayed consistently good, and I was very popular among my classmates. The histrionic personality traits that I exhibited were not interfering with my ability to function. Was I eccentric? Yes. Was I ill? No.

So, there I was, in my middle teens, covering my bedroom walls with things I found on the street, adding to my collection of a vast assortment of decorative items and objects, listening to cassette tapes of albums from the 1980's, singing along to Cindy Lauper's 'She's So Unusual', as though nothing in the whole wide world was more *natural* than me doing the things I did. That was when I began my highly formative friendship with two enigmatic characters in my life story. Their names were Car and Lev. And, they soon became my beloved 'Twins of Muse'.

A TASTE OF INSANITY

CHAPTER 7

SO, AFTER THE TREK PROGRAM, I TRANSFERRED TO KITSILANO Secondary School, joining my little brother in the public schooling institution just a few blocks down from where we lived with our mother. That was where I would spend grades eleven and twelve, accumulating excellent grades, running cross-country, and playing soccer on the district team called the Point Grey Panthers.

On the first day of class, I realized that Car, a girl I'd attended Ideal Mini School with, was also a student at Kits. We renewed our friendship, only just before she introduced me to her best friend, Lev. But, after a week or so of grade eleven, both Car and Lev dropped out and started home-schooling. They encouraged me to join them, but I insisted on staying at the mainstream high school, to mingle with the 1400 or so students there.

Now, my bizarre style of dressing continued, and I started a hat collection. I remember riding my banana board down the street to school in the morning, wearing a sombrero, and being remarkably comfortable drawing attention to myself. Car and Lev and I would spend a good part of each day, visiting. Lev soon became my girlfriend, and the three of us bonded, as elitist snobs exiled from the masses. We studied the drawings of Brian Froud, and dabbled in Wiccan magic, spending dark nights at the nearby waterfall, conducting ceremonies in the name of the lord and lady. They were my muses, and they impressed me to no end.

Going to school everyday was rather stressful, in hindsight, as just about every teenager can attest. But, I made it my livelihood, and I'm proud to say that I was never late or absent that whole year. Right around then, I hung out with my brother's friends and smoked pot just about every weekend. I had made several one-of-a-kind pipes when I was at Rainbow Lake the previous summer, and I called them Gandalf pipes because they were long and crooked like those belonging to a wizard. I didn't like pipe tobacco much, but I was smoking a strange mixture of mullein, sage, yarrow, and kinnickinnick. Who knows what all those chemicals were doing to my developing brain?

Soon, wearing these old leather boots, on the heels of which Car had painted a portrait of the Japanese goddess of lightning, I remember being in grade eleven art class one day, when a somewhat pivotal event occurred. The art teacher was out of the room briefly, and my classmates and I were just working on our art projects, and we all got talking. I was seated at the same table as my friend. She was the only other kid at school who also had a mohawk. I told her my last name was 'Ditmars' because my family and I were from Mars. She laughed. Then, I told her that the lump at the base of my skull was there because that's where they had implanted the microchip. She laughed again.

Only, she was laughing because that's what teenagers do. No one else in the classroom heard what I had said, except for her. And, this is why I feel as though I am truly doing a service when I present my life story to high school students. Because, if only the BC Schizophrenia Society had come to my high school and told us about what the warning signs of the illness were, my friend may have gone to the teacher or the counsellor or the principal or my parents, and I might have been properly assessed and treated, then, thereby averting the many emergency situations that arose in my early twenties. Maybe, I could have received the help I needed.

For, in those days, I was viewed as eccentric, or precocious, or queer, but not crazy. However, I remember sometime in grade eleven, writing one of my latest books at my desk in my bedroom. I was listening to David Bowie's music, and I had a candle burning.

Suddenly, I heard a voice that seemed to be channeling through the filter of my psychic awareness: *Paranoia will solidify.* Of course, I quickly wrote it down on paper, because it seemed to be such a magical experience. The book I was writing was a short novel about a futuristic colony on Mars.

I heard a knock at the door. It was my mom, checking up on me. We talked for a few minutes, before, from out of nowhere, I told her that I wished I could have a taste of insanity. She was very disturbed by this, as any mother would be. But, I was very sincere.

Like just about every person on this planet, my mother had had a direct connection to someone with psychosis. Her mother's sister's son had developed schizophrenia early on in his life, and died at the tender young age of 25. It had been suicide. Unaware of this, seeing as my mother had never mentioned this story to me, there I was, wanting to experience a little bit of what it might be like to experience madness. I was guilty of romanticizing craziness, to my mother's very personal detriment.

Eleventh grade was very enjoyable, for the most part. I was enrolled in a creative writing class that consisted of mostly grade twelve students. The entire class went to a writing retreat on Gambier Island for a weekend workshop. It was fun. We scattered into various places in the old growth forests, and tackled the beast known as stream-of-consciousness, with naive and ambitious hopes of finding ourselves. Later that evening, we sat around the fireplace, sharing what we had written.

Now, soon after, during Christmas break, I was at Rainbow Lake Ranch, back in the world of kerosene lamps and wood stoves, when I took it upon myself to write an epic poem. It was inspired by the Mayan prophecy about the end of the world. And, even before writing the first word, I knew the exact structure. It would be two thousand and twelve quatrains of rhyming iambic tetrameter. I knew it in my heart of hearts. I knew it like I knew my own name.

Come grade twelve, I was still very close to my muses, Car and Lev. One weekend, Car met me and Lev at the waterfall. She had a treasure with her. I was her dad's old pipe. It was carved so that the bowl looked like a woman's face. Wandering around the seawall, Car and Lev and I dreamed dreams, and explored the endless labyrinth of life. I was a hundred percent certain that I was the reincarnation of Fredriech Neitzche.

Eventually, I was writing non-stop, with a plethora of ideas and abstract concepts rushing through my head. I was on the honour roll, and every single elective I took was in some form of art or another. My brother dropped out of grade ten, and went to live at Rainbow Lake, to do home-schooling with dad and Jen. By the time I graduated from secondary school, I had tried LSD three times.

INHALING A MOLECULE
OF THE DALAI LAMA'S FARTS
CHAPTER 8

CHRISTMAS HAS COME AND GONE. AND, THE NEW YEAR IS FAST approaching. Tomorrow is January 1st. Or, as I like to call it: December 32nd. It seems, no matter which medication I'm on or which dosage is prescribed, I will probably always have a tendency to look at things differently than most people.

His Holiness, the Dalai Lama believes that life is suffering, and that every single human being suffers. If I use mental illness as an example, it becomes really very interesting. In Canada, the official diagnostics manual lists approximately three hundred mental illnesses. A fraction of Canadians suffers from maybe one or two of them, and the rest of the population is without mental afflictions. But, Buddhism says otherwise.

I have heard that, according to Buddhist philosophy, there are sixty-four thousand mental illnesses, and every single human being suffers from a huge array of several of these. The implications of this teaching is that all human beings are put in the same boat, together. It inspires compassion, and implies a sense of mutual, collective, even universal, suffering. We are all here on this planet, suffering together, and in sync.

Like many people, I see a psychiatrist regularly. And, I know how it feels to be a passenger on a crowded city bus, when my cell phone rings, I answer, the person on the other end of the line asks me what I'm doing, and I reply, telling them that I am on my way to see my shrink. The stares are almost inevitable. People sitting next to me get up and move further away. The stigma is almost palpable.

Do I know why this is? No. Do I have a hunch as to how to reduce stigma? Yes. If everyone in the world were to be diagnosed with multiple mental afflictions, and if we all saw a psychiatrist regularly, and if we all took responsibility for maintaining our own mental health, we could eradicate stigma and *simultaneously* avoid crisis situations, because the quality and quantity of our suffering could be monitored and measured, preventing both breakdowns and relapses. We are all one. Everything is connected. The air we breathe is shared by all of us. Energy cannot be created nor destroyed, only transformed. The cells in my body were at one time, millions of years ago, belonging to a dinosaur. On a molecular level, each and every sentient being is sharing the same air. Who needs an autograph of a celebrity to feel connected to something important? Isn't it enough to know, in our heart of hearts, that we are breathing the gases that once belonged in the bowels of the Dalai Lama himself?

My sincerest apologies for the crudeness of this metaphor. But, it's true. All is One. The mystics knew this intuitively, thousands of years ago, and physicists are only now catching up with the realizations of this universal wisdom.

Every day that passes, I am rediscovering my true nature. This Christmas, however, I did not struggle with my delusions of being the messiah. My uncle and aunt are visiting from Toronto, and it has been good to visit with them. And, a couple days ago, my son, Gabriel, was passing through Vancouver. In the middle of the night, there was an earthquake. It woke me up out of a dead sleep, and I wondered if it was God's way of warning me.

So, there I was, in my bed, lying down, under the warm blankets, feeling the shaking of the fragile Earth. At first, I thought it was just the guy upstairs in one of his midnight fits. But, then I knew what it was. The jolting sensation wasn't enough to prevent me from going right back to sleep (thanks be to the miracle of mainstream pharmaceutical anti-psychotic medication!) And, the following day, I heard on the radio that it was most definitely an earthquake. 4.8 magnitude! The first one here in over a decade.

Sweet were the grapes I tasted last night, when I was over at my mother's house for dinner. And, sweet was the visit. Today, I am going to invite my uncle and aunt over to my apartment, so they can see my place and view the BCSS videos on my computer. Sunlight is pouring through my window, as I write this.

In the process of composing my memoir, I am filled with an unmistakable sense of self-reflection. The provincial co-ordinator for the BCSS has always taken every opportunity to comment to our scholastic audience as to just how able I am to reflect upon myself and gain insight into my illness. As I said before, anosognosia (lack of insight) plagues the majority of schizophrenics. You might think this is a good thing, something for which I should be thankful, but my doctor disagrees.

At a recent appointment with my psychiatrist, he was playing the devil's advocate, saying that the lack of insight is a blessing in disguise. He argues that it is more pleasant to be oblivious. According to him, I am unfortunate to know when and how I suffer. But, I know better. Ignorance is *not* bliss.

How am I going to feel when I wake up tomorrow morning, to herald in the new year? First of all, I will be well rested. I always make a point to get ten or eleven hours of sleep every night. And, New Year's Eve will be no exception. Sleeping well, eating well, and staying active are three basic strategies I've developed, as a way to care for my brain. I will wake up tomorrow morning, the same way I wake up every morning: looking forward to what the day has to hold.

COMING OF AGE IN
A COLLEGE OF THE OCCULT
CHAPTER 9

EVENTUALLY, I GRADUATED FROM HIGH SCHOOL IN JUNE OF 1997. AT the tender young age of eighteen, I was being beckoned ever forth by the elusive muse of adulthood, trying to make sense out of this military industrial society and, most importantly, how it pertained to me. I knew I was an artist. I knew I was a writer. I knew that I was inspired. But, what I didn't know was where I belonged.

Positioned on a chair in the second row, on the stage of the Orpheum, I was daydreaming, looking up at the ceiling, musing over the images described in the painting mural where colourful hues captivated my keen eye. Suddenly, the girl next to me nudged me. And, I heard my name being called. Coming back down to earth, I realized that my art teacher, Mr. Roberts, was giving me an award. It was the fine arts award. So, shuffling carefully down the long row of seats, I made my way up to the podium, and graciously accepted the plaque and a cheque for two hundred and fifty dollars. No speech.

I was coming of age. I got my driver's licence, lost my virginity, bought and drank alcohol, made several startling fashion statements along the way, and now I had graduated from grade twelve. But, my mind was elsewhere. I was focussed on finding myself.

Previously, Car and Lev and Reuben and I had stumbled across a small paper flyer in one of Crowley's books, on the shelves at Banyen. It was an advertisement for The Hermetic Order of The Golden Dawn, a self-proclaimed 'college of the occult'. There was listed the address and the phone number. Of course, we called the number, and left a message. A middle-aged man by the name of Bear returned our call, and left a message on my mother's answering machine. Soon, it was arranged that the four of us would go to Gastown, and attend an 'orientation meeting' at the Golden Dawn temple house, at 132 Powell street. We learned about the grade structure, and got some of our questions answered, and took part in some fairly advanced holotrophic breathing techniques. My brother and the muses thought it was funny. But, I was genuinely attracted to the idea of being a member of the order.

However, first, before signing up, I moved to Rainbow Lake to write. On July 9th, I sat down at my desk, by the window in the downstairs room of the old log house, with two lanterns warmly aglow, ready to write my next epic. With my pen poised hovering over the page, I looked over my shoulder to my left, and saw what seemed to be a name, cryptically inscribed on the surface of the log wall. *Maya.* Then, after visually hallucinating, I heard a voice, which I assumed was the voice of Maya, the goddess of Illusion. She proceeded to dictate the entirety of what turned out to be a 250, 000 word poem of rhyming iambic pentameter.

And, there I was. Finding myself. I had signed up for a position in the Arts One Program at UBC. So, just before Labour Day, early in September, I made my way back to Vancouver, to attend university. I survived one week. It was overwhelming, so I dropped out. The last thing I wanted was to be lost among the masses. I was inspired. Then, returning to Rainbow Lake, I compiled my writings, and continued working on my latest epic narrative.

Now and then, I would make a trip to the city, for this reason or that. The first and perhaps the most memorable visit was for the purpose of my initiation into the first grade of the order, Neophyte 0=0, on October 10th. These days, I regard that day as my spiritual birthday. And, I was eager to share my poem to my new brothers and sisters at the temple. We were bound by the oath of secrecy, so my family had no idea what I was actually up to. As far as my brother and parents knew, I was writing and making art, and visiting with my new friends. Then, I fell in love with Sunflower, who was my first teacher. She was two grades ahead of me, and I remember bringing gifts to class and leaving them discreetly on her table. I was eighteen, and she was twenty-two. The love I felt for her was like none other. My relationship with Lev was old news, and I was infatuated with my new love as though I were under a spell.

Yet, it was also very daunting. Sunflower and I would write letter after letter, expressing our mutual love, and she expressed an interest in travelling to Rainbow Lake to visit me. I was writing page after page of my poem, that autumn. And, in November, something magical happened. I was returning to my house by the creek, after a week of work as a carpenter's helper in Anahim Lake, when I heard something. It sounded like a squeal. I followed the sounds, and found, to my surprise, that the barn cat had given birth to seven kittens, down in the basement. At the time, I was writing the part of the poem in which the seven main characters (angels) were becoming archangels. So, I named the seven kittens: *Gabriel, Samael, Raphael, Sachiel, Auriel, Cassiel,* and *Michael.*

FOOTPRINTS OF
A DRUNKEN ANGEL
CHAPTER 10

WITH HIGH SCHOOL BEHIND ME, I FOUND MYSELF DRUNK ON THE WINE of life. Each and every day at the ranch, I was ecstatic to have discovered the world of occult magic (with the Golden Dawn) and the power of true love (with Sunflower). I was tipsy with enlightenment, inspired to create, and happy to be writing epic poetry. It had not yet occurred to me that writing epic poetry in a world of two-minute attention spans is a bit like being a butcher in a world comprised of only vegetarians. None-the-less, I was content in my soul's naivety.

Horizons of trees, fields, and winter snow crowned my awareness, and I meditated daily on the magical ceremonies taught by the order. As for the kittens, I fed them with a bottle every few hours. Then, I realized that keeping all of them was, very simply, not an option. So, I brought them outside into the cold, hoping they would survive the mid-winter temperatures. All seven of them, huddled together to keep warm, occupied a corner of one of the old abandoned cow-barns. I went to sleep that night with fingers crossed.

In the morning, I went over to the cow barn, only to discover that they were freezing to death. Six of them were moving slowly. The seventh was not moving at all. I was devastated. Quickly, I brought them all into my house where it was warm.

The one that died was the one I had named Raphael. Suddenly, I remembered that this was my brother's middle name, and I feared the worst: that this was an omen from God warning me that my brother was destined to die. I buried Raphael beneath a pine tree.

Eventually, the kittens recovered, all save the one. It was then that I chose to adopt the black and white one, whom I had named Gabriel. She was one of the larger ones, and had a white patch on the centre of her forehead. It looked like a star, located where the third eye would be. And, once I decided to keep her as my familiar, I recalled my high school fascination with that name. All over my school binders in grade twelve, I had drawn the sigil of the angel of the moon, as though in a sort of trance. Gabriel was a name to which I was attracted. Still am.

Now, during that December, I was immersed in the art and science of Jewish mysticism. The Qabalah opened my eyes to the light in the darkness. On a daily basis, I spent the hours writing at my desk up in the attic. In fact, soon, I turned the entire attic into a temple. I used old cardboard oat barrels as altars, and I painted a magic circle on the floor. I called it Temple Calliope (after the muse of epic poetry).

I also spent hours every day, performing the Lesser Banishing Ritual of the Pentagram (LBRP). And, I also performed the Middle Pillar Ritual (MPR), and the Comfort Ritual (CR). The four archangels of the elements were present in my sanctuary, and I meditated on them throughout each day. I was beginning to walk the straight and narrow path towards my higher self.

God was to be found in LOTU (Lord Of The Universe), and I had yet to comprehend it. The thing that kept me sane in those dark days was the love I felt for my girlfriend. Sunflower wrote me many long love letters, and I replied to each and every one of them. Some were written in calligraphy, and some were accompanied by photos of Renaissance paintings, and some included copies of *The Beak*, which was the monthly newsletter of our temple (Temple Tehuti). Sunflower also sent me grade material pertaining to Neophyte o=o.

Her love was mine, and my love was hers. We also talked weekly, on the radio phone, and discussed plans for her to visit me in the wilderness sometime in the new year. But, she had to run it by her business partner first, before making any solid plans. She and her partner owned and operated an art gallery located right next door to the temple. They were both sorors (sisters) in the order, and were both a couple grades ahead of me.

Then, in the dead of winter, when dark were all the days, I made a journey to Vancouver.

THE LAST CAR ON THE HIGHWAY
CHAPTER 11

THE JOURNEY WAS EPIC. IT WAS IN HONOUR OF THREE THINGS: SEEING Sunflower again, being initiated into Zelator 1=10, and last but not least, finding homes for the kittens. Epic, as in endless. Epic, as in full circle. And, epic, as in a tireless attempt to defy the laws of nature.

Hierophant, Hierus, and Hegemon, along with all of the other temple officers, in full ritual attire, were waiting for me in Vancouver's most eclectic and profound warehouse rental unit, two blocks down from Main and Hastings, where prostitutes, pimps, junkies, and johns prowled the alleyway. So, early one sunny cold January morning, my father accompanied me down to where the car was kept.

Easily minus twenty degrees, outside, the rusty old station wagon was frozen solid. We spent two hours trying to warm the engine so that it would start. Finally, we got it so that the engine started with a gentle turn of the key. I said goodbye to dad, and started off on my way.

But, shortly before arriving at Anahim Lake, I drove into a ditch, walked the rest of the way into town, begged the guy at the garage to help me out with his tow truck, and eventually arrived at the restaurant, where I had lunch. Realizing that I had a flat tire, I put on the spare, and headed off down the highway in the direction of Williams Lake. With the cats in the car, it became something greater than myself. I had to find them homes, attend the initiation, and see my girlfriend in the city.

Outside the moving station wagon, which was gliding over the snow, the air was chilled and the skies were black. Then, I got lost. I was on one of the roads near Chimney Lake, where I was hoping to spend the night with one of Jen's friends. As I rolled up and down driveways looking for the right house, there were meows and hisses in the background. After many brushes with death along the treacherous roads, I asked to use the phone at one of the local residences. They told me to stay away, while they made the call.

Old Sophia, a friend of mine as well, agreed to let me spend the night. She met me on the road, when it started to snow heavily. I remember the snowflakes, the size of quarters, pummelling down ahead of me onto the windshield, looking like something out of Star Wars or something. I grew anxious.

Kind Sophia, whom I had known since I was a kid growing up in Strathcona, she took me in, made me a cup of tea, and fed me a batch of midnight waffles and maple syrup. Her house was full of cats, so she didn't hesitate in letting me bring my feline companions indoors for the night. I slept for twelve hours. Then, around noon, realizing I had slept away a good part of the day, I asked her if I could spend another night. She agreed.

On that afternoon, she let me borrow one of her books, called "The Story of San Michel". I set off the next morning, slowly, having wrestled relentlessly with the engine of the car. Finally, I got it started, loaded the cages into the back, and headed south towards Hope. What made matters worse, there was a blizzard and my windshield wipers weren't working all that well. Moving at a snail's pace, I was the last car on the highway. The huge semi-trucks were honking and passing and sending mud in the direction of my face. It was horrible. I contemplated death. But, what kept me from fearing death was that my epic poem was unfinished, and I thought what a tragedy it would have been had I never been able to finish it. But, I made it to Hope, where I checked into one of the cheap motels. Once again, the snowflakes were the size of quarters.

From Hope to Vancouver, the roads were good the following day. So, I was happy. Then, with half-melted snow on the roof of the car, I parked on Powell street, in front of the temple. I had arrived just in time for the 1=10 initiation. The cage of cats was temporarily at my mom's house.

Like I had hoped, Sunflower was still as beautiful as when I had last seen her. She supervised my grade advancement examination, and stayed around with me for the post-initiation potluck party, where I recited for her the entirety of Ginsberg's poem, "Howl". She was impressed, and I was proud.

Orations of the world, the words spoken by the officers at the temple were written by W.B. Yeats, for the most part, especially the more poetic parts of the hundred year old script. I was only in Zelator back then, but I passionately intended to be an officer someday in the future. Being a practicing magician, I had been granted a great responsibility. Several times during that visit to the city, I used the fully functioning Solomonic temple, complete with altars, pillars, veils, candles, and incense, invoking the element of Earth, meditating, and breathing.

Voices, visions, vast realms of otherworldly entities, and ancient mythical symbolism revealed something that I had never before seen. I learned the grade material which I had been given access to, and fell deeper in love with Sunflower. I found homes for the cats (Car took five, and I adopted Gabriel). Then, I eventually made it back to Rainbow Lake to continue writing my poem.

Eternity and Chronos (king and queen respectively) commanded that their seven children, the angelic archetypes of the seven ancient planets, descend to Earth and save mankind. Around Christmas time around the turn of the millennium, Gabriel, Samael, Raphael, Sachiel, Auriel, Cassiel, and Michael land in a garbage dumpster in a back alley of east Los Angeles. Needless to say, I was processing my own life, and I spent that winter and spring writing obsessively.

PLEASE IGNORE
THESE COFFEE-STAINS
CHAPTER 12

RELUCTANTLY, I AM SCHEDULED TO MOVE OUT OF THIS ONE BEDROOM apartment where I've been living for the past fifteen months or so. But, every day that goes by, now as we enter the year of 2016, I face the bittersweet reminder that this *is* mental health housing after all.

A guy who lives in the apartment above my suite is moderately to severely disturbed. It must be some form of Tourettes or something. Cause, whatever it is that he suffers from, his behaviour is frightening at times. Randomly, he screams the same thing over and over again.

Now, I have considered knocking on his door, to request that he settle down a bit. But, I lack the courage. Besides which, I don't think it would do any good because I don't think he does it consciously. Strange. And, what's even stranger is that he seems perfectly normal at the weekly meetings. Every Tuesday afternoon, all the residents in this building meet in the lounge and discuss things. He seems rational and social, and what is even more surprising, he is articulate and intelligent. I don't know what to do.

The building manager knows about this, and has notified the man's case worker. Apparently, he's moving out soon, into the community. I wish him all the best. Hopefully, his new place is not somewhere in which he would be evicted due to his disturbing behaviour. It must be really something, to be him.

I actually get it. I get the distinction that has to be made, the distinction between a person and a person's illness. God knows I've been on the wrong side of *that* skewer of stigma and social prejudice. When an individual is sick with a cold, he is not blamed for sneezing. When an individual is sick with a stomach flu, he is not blamed for throwing up. Likewise, when I was violent due to psychosis years ago, society was compassionate and insightful enough to deem me not criminally responsible.

Now, also in this building, there are addicts. Same thing. When they do something 'crazy' because of intoxication, is it the drug or is the person? This debate will probably continue for as long as the human race exists. It's a human dilemma.

God knows I've been plagued with voices and visions. And, my psychiatrist says that these hallucinations will probably follow me to the grave. But, when I die, my tombstone will say that here died a happy man. And, I do not doubt that there will be many flowers falling atop the soil.

So, there you have it.

Not knowing something is due to one of two things: innocence or ignorance. We can blame the ignorant, but we cannot blame the innocent. The King Of Chronic Insomnia and I have explored this topic to no end. At my place, or at his place, over coffee or lunch, he and I have discussed how the broken tool of 'lack of knowledge' is indeed a two-pronged fork. There are people who have never been informed, and there are the people who have and yet they chose to disregard the information. The folly of the fool is not the madness of the magician.

Right now, in my life, I am a bit of an addict myself. I have become completely dependant on three medications: benztropine, risperidone and olanzapine. Also, apart from this concoction of medicine, I am addicted to nicotine and caffeine. I suppose it could be worse.

A nice cup of coffee in the morning and a few puffs on my vaporizer are what keeps me going. When my friends and I visited on Saturday at the local cafe, we did our usual coffee fix. Normally, the three of us meet on Friday afternoon, but it was New Year's Day, so the cafe was closed. It certainly required a concerted effort on our part to adjust to the break from routine, but we managed.

Vicariously, my lifestyle is fairly healthy. I limit myself to two or three cups of coffee per day. But, my nicotine use is difficult to measure. As my dad always says: *whatever works*. There is, however, a clear distinction that must be properly made between use and abuse. Anything can be used, and therefor anything can be abused. I'm just glad I stayed far away from harder drugs like cocaine and heroin.

I am having a good new year so far. Today is the 6th of January. 2016 has arrived. Normally, I would be taking my Wednesday client to a yoga class, but he called the team to cancel because he's not feeling well. Apparently, cancellations go along with the territory. So, after years of being a peer support worker, I'm getting used to it.

Now, I'm back to work this week. Both of my Monday clients showed up, and the visits went well. Yesterday, the big event was yet another presentation of my life story to the students at UBC School of Nursing. And, I'm proud to say that the talk was one of the best ones yet. No mutism. No thought-blockage. And, no poverty of speech. Just a really good connection, and successful articulation with an ample amount of spontaneity. They had some really good questions afterwards. And, I was speaking for almost an hour.

Good for me. But, oddly enough, during the fifteen minute break between speakers, when I visited the bathroom down the hall from the classroom, I hallucinated profoundly. I often hear voices while urinating. Either that, or while I'm waking up or falling asleep. The most recent auditory hallucination I had while falling asleep was bizarre. It sounded a lot like tuning into a radio station that was just a little bit off the correct station. It sounded like static and muffled voices. The moment that I heard it, I experienced a moderate flood of adrenalin rushing through my veins, and my heartbeat became fast.

So, life goes on. Today is the first day of the rest of this incarnation.

COLLIDING WITH MY HIGHER GENIUS

CHAPTER 13

THE ORDER OF THE GOLDEN DAWN, APART FROM THE EVIDENT BRAIN-washing that was said to occur, proved to be my chosen path. I had signed the vow, so I was obligated to refrain from telling anyone about my involvement. The penalty for dispensing any information regarding the existence of the order or the names of its members was described in the oath I took. The threat was that of insanity, serious injury, or death.

Huge was the body of the international organization, mainly spanning across the countries of Europe and North America. I was a part of something big. And, the purpose of the secret society was to transform the initiated individual into something truly great. The initiations, rituals, meditations, invocations, and banishings were all designed as a way to systematically unite the initiate with his or her holy guardian angel. My higher self (or higher genius) was never more than an arm's length away, figuratively. I was already well on my way towards self-actualization.

Earlier on, just prior to my Neophyte initiation, when I signed the vow, I was given my power name. I was to be known as *Frater Superbus Animus.*

My motto was *Exalted Breath.* It resonated quite well with me, at first. But, those days as a Zelator were just the beginning.

Under the spell of love, I invited Sunflower and Shakespeare (my two best friends in the temple community) to come visit me at Rainbow Lake. Shakespeare, two years younger than me but two grades ahead of me, arrived in the early spring. He and I had a wonderful visit, complete with my recital of Gibran's opus book (which I had memorized), and several scrying sessions using my crystal ball. Sunflower came later, for the month of June. She and I made love, wrote, painted, swam in the creek, bathed in moonlight, and made our daily visits to the attic of my log cabin to do ritual work.

New to the order, and equally new to the prospect of sexual intimacy, I was nineteen times around the sun, and only beginning to realize my spiritual potential.

I was preparing myself for the upcoming magical conference that was scheduled to take place in Los Angeles the first week of August, 1998. So, after spending over a month in the forests of Rainbow Lake, she and I descended from heaven and arrived in the Vancouver alleyways of the downtown east-side, where we reconvened with our brothers and sisters at the temple house.

Verse upon verse, I completed my second epic poem on July 9th, after exactly one year of writing. And, paragraph upon paragraph, I continued to study the grade material. I was now in the grade known as Theoricus 2=9.

Eventually, several of us packed ourselves in the back of a big white van, and drove to California, where Power Week was going to be held. We drove non-stop, from Vancouver to L.A.. It took us twenty-one hours. We had no air conditioning in the vehicle, so we sweated most of the way there, gunning it down the highways through Washington and Oregon. The Mad Scientist, Lotus Noesis, Shakespeare, Sunflower and I arrived in the parking lot just outside the entrance to the mother temple, somewhere in a hidden location in a commercial zone of Orange County. As we stumbled out of the sliding door of the van, we were greeted by several brothers and sisters. They smiled at us, and traced pentagrams which they projected in our general direction.

Rare esoteric subject matter, all five grade advancement ceremonies, classes on various magical techniques, and endless group meditations, all combined in a cute little package, presented itself to my young and impressionable mind.

Soon, having had a great time, we drove back to Temple Tehuti, and did our very best to process and digest the experiences we had had in the states. For the other brothers and sisters, it was a return home, a return to work, and a return to crazy Canada. But, for Sunflower and me, it was a very intense time in our relationship, seeing as she had decided to come live with me on the ranch.

Eventually, with all her worldly possessions packed in the back of our station wagon, we returned to Rainbow Lake, where we were going to take care of the property while my father went to work as a carpenter in Vancouver for the winter. This position as 'care-taker' was actually going to be time for the two of us to spend writing, reading, studying, and meditating on our holy guardian angels. Gabriel, the little black and white kitten, slept with us, and kept the mice away from the house. Sunflower and I fed the horses, dogs, cats and chickens, and stocked up on firewood while the temperature of the autumn air grew chill.

STOOP NOT DOWN
CHAPTER 14

NEITHER ONE OF US, SUNFLOWER NOR I, KNEW WHAT WE WERE getting into. The studies, the rituals, the meditations, the entire astral current of the G.D., complete with divine names and secret handshakes, it seeming all so endurable and permanent. But, living at Rainbow Lake was intense. We were not spiritually prepared.

And, on Friday, November 13th, 1998, I was astrally initiated into Practicus 3=8. Sunflower was right there by my side, ready and willing to answer any of my questions, seeing as she was in Philosophus 4=7. So, there we were, me in the grade of water, and her in the grade of fire, taking care of the animals, and baking our own bread in the wood stoves. We made our daily way circumambulating around the magic circle in Temple Calliope.

My books were coming along nicely, and her paintings, canvas after canvas, were revealing themselves splendidly. While I meditated on the undines, Sunflower meditated on the salamanders. And, soon winter came, along with snow and ice.

Early one morning, we received three visitors. Anahim Lake's one and only police officer, along with two local ranchers, came to our house on snowmobiles. It was frightening, really. The knock at the door. They came inside to warm up and make sure we were doing alright. We were just glad they didn't come while one of us was in the middle of a magical ceremony upstairs.

Soon, after sipping coffee from the thermoses they had brought, they got back on their machines and bid us farewell. Sunflower breathed a deep sigh of relief, knowing they had gone. I even saw her wipe the sweat from off her brow.

From then on in, she painted furiously, and I wrote feverishly, all winter long. The books that I had composed began to pile up. We collaborated on a few projects, and shared in a mutual artistic camaraderie. Sunflower and I shared the same bed at night, but our level of physical intimacy diminished down to nothing.

Ordinarily, I did most of the cooking and chores. After all, technically, I was her host. I didn't mind the fact that the majority of responsibility fell upon my shoulders. It was an idyllic lifestyle, which I sincerely enjoyed.

Reading and re-reading the initiations, especially the speeches delivered by the three main officers, I was Sunflower's closest Frater, and she was my closest Soror. We were haunted by the words of W.B. Yeats, and did our very best to *stoop not down.*

The winter came and went, as we made monthly visits to the post office. But, one day, we were shocked to see that the postmistress had opened and resealed one of our letters. It was an information booklet from the Rosicrucians.

Horrified to know that someone in town had been informed as to our esoteric interests, we felt violated by the discriminatory redneck small town mentality. But, we reluctantly concluded that the prejudice which was being placed on us was inevitable. I still don't know what the postmistress actually thought of us, though there were some filthy looks.

Early spring, the snow began to melt, and the season of ice-fishing on the lake was over. The end of our stay in the forest was very soon in sight. The question as to whether or not Sunflower was still my 'girlfriend' crossed my mind. She hadn't kissed me in months. But, both she and I felt that our time spent at Rainbow Lake had been time well spent. We made plans to move back to the city.

Now, early on in 1999, my dad returned from work, and thanked us for care-taking. Turning responsibility over to him, Sunflower and I made the long trip back to Vancouver. The temple house awaited our arrival, along with all our brothers and sisters in the Great Work.

And, returning to civilization in style, I joined my mother and brother amidst a crowd at a sold out concert featuring Paul Simon and Bob Dylan. The usher at GM Place yelled over the noise right into my ear that I looked like Jesus. I was dressed in a navy blue set of baggy kung fu pants and a long black bathrobe and sandals. I suppose that with my long hair and beard, the usher was absolutely correct.

My return to Vancouver was a bit of a culture shock. It sent me and Sunflower in opposite directions. She moved in with one of the adepts, and I rented a room at the temple house. With barely enough space for a bed and a desk, my room was the smallest of the lot.

Entering Tehuti again, returning to the traditional Solomonic symbolism of colour-coded elemental altars, black and white pillars, and a checkered tile floor, I was in a state of flux and transformation. I tried to look composed and rational, while deep inside I was mourning the loss of the woman whom I had previously called my girlfriend.

Like water off a duck's back, the emotions of archangel Gabriel bathed me with a glory never to be witnessed by any mortal man. My feline familiar remained at the ranch. But, the archangelic essence indicative of Practicus was very much present in my life. I got a job as a carpenter, along with The Mad Scientist. That lasted a day. Then, I was invited to come work at a commercial art studio where they made decorative tiles.

Eventually, I was hired there, being paid minimum wage, thanks to The Scarab, who got me the job. It was profound. The Scarab was Tehuti's acting Hierophant, and The Mad Scientist was Tehuti's acting Hierus. The three of us worked 9-5 five days a week, pouring plaster.

Soon, the temple house and all of its residents (four French-Canadians and myself) were gearing up for Power Week '99, which was scheduled to be held in Vancouver. Lotus Noesis and I were both in Practicus and both teaching Neophyte every Monday evening.

Sunflower and I were very distant, during those first few months back in the city. I heard a rumour that she was seen at a rave party high on magic mushrooms. As for me, I was making an attempt at walking the straight and narrow way, on a path somewhere between Boaz and Yachin (the pillar of cloud and the pillar of flame respectively). I was well on my way to uniting with my holy guardian angel. The temple was a warehouse in Blood Alley, but it could not have felt more sublime.

SHAKING HANDS WITH THE GREATLY HONOURED CHIEF

CHAPTER 15

THE NECESSARY PREPARATIONS WERE MADE, AND AUGUST WAS FAST approaching. That meant Power Week '99, with all the brothers and sisters at Temple Tehuti making arrangements to host about a hundred members from around the world. The Air was electric.

Horizon to horizon, the sun rose and set there, in the downtown east side, where pimps and prostitutes and junkies prowled the alleys, not suspecting for a moment that behind the door in Gastown there was a gathering of magicians being held. I was working hard at the commercial art studio, and teaching Neophyte class every Monday night with Lotus Noesis.

Eventually, the visiting members arrived, and we did our best to billet them. I wrote and slept in my cubby-hole of a room, situated between the larger temple and the smaller temple. It was cozy.

On the first day of Power Week, I was walking down the hallway that led from the office past the main temple towards the housing quarters that were situated in the back. There, in front of my bedroom door, I saw the Greatly Honoured Chief. He was looking at my paintings.

My hands reached toward him, and we performed the order's secret handshake, in the form of a figure-eight, complete with eye contact and three consecutive downward motions. It was the first time I had ever met him in person. The Chief was middle aged, with a shaven head, and seemed somehow too normal. But, I was impressed.

Eventually, after many group rituals and classes, it came time for my physical initiation into Practicus 3=8. But, there was a problem. One of the officers was absent. So, on Thursday night, I went into my initiation into Philosophus 4=7. And, backwards, out of order, my first physical initiation into Practicus 3=8 was scheduled for the Friday. So, physically, I went from Neophyte to Zelator to Theoricus to Philosophus and then backwards to Practicus. It was very upsetting, but was unavoidable.

Glowing still, then in the midnight hours, the candles were burning, and I was alive. Then, came my time to shine. I organized a recital of one of my poems to be held in the small temple beside my bedroom.

And, what a great way for me to connect with our visiting members! Afterwards, the Greatly Honoured Chief gave a last minute lecture to everyone in the large temple. He mentioned the word 'Epiphany', the title of my poem. Shakespeare had many intelligent questions for the man, all of which were answered truly and thoroughly.

Divinely inspired, I was now an Honoured Frater. Then, as I entered Philosophus, Sunflower, my estranged girlfriend, entered the grade of Portal and received the white sash. I was very proud of her. She was seeming so strong and beautiful. I wasn't sure where she was living or what she was doing for work, but it didn't matter. I could tell she was surviving our breakup, as gorgeous and as radiant as ever. Whether or not she knew it, I still loved her very deeply. We had shared an intimate winter in the middle of nowhere, and no one could ever take that away from us.

Entering the grade of fire, I was excited by life. After Power Week '99, working a nine to five job, studying every Friday and teaching every Monday, I only had to walk a block and a half to visit my little brother. Reuben was living with a bunch of artists and musicians in the lobby of the Roosevelt Hotel.

And, living there, that fall, he and his friends built a stage out of twenty-six doors which the hotel manager was throwing away. And, they planned to invite punk rock bands to perform at their place, charging tickets at the door.

To add to the ambience, I stayed up all night one time, on a ladder, painting a huge mural on the wall above the stage. It was a portrait of the Virgin Mary holding a sunflower at her heart, superimposed with two giant hands pointing at one another (a la Michelangelo's sistine chapel).

However, one morning as I left the temple house on my way to work, exiting the back door that led into the alley, my whole world changed. I saw a bumper sticker on the side of the dumpster. The bumper sticker read: *Repent Sinner.* Then, I walked a few paces further, and found another bumper sticker. *Repent Sinner.* And, then another one, and another one, situated every ten feet or so. It was *Repent Sinner Repent Sinner Repent Sinner...* all the way to Science World, precisely along the exact course I took to get to work each morning. Suddenly, I felt sure that I was being watched. Monitored. Observed. Under surveillance. Persecuted!

IT'S GOTTA COME FROM ME
CHAPTER 16

TODAY, I WAS PLANNING TO GO TO THE SUNSHINE COAST TO VISIT MY son. But, I'm realizing that there are a few things I need to do here, like laundry, grocery shopping, and some paper work. It's a long way to Gibsons, two hours there and two hours back. All that traveling in one day would bring me home well after dark. And, anyone who knows me well remembers that I'm not good after sunset. I get distracted by points of light. So, I'm not going to make the trip today, even though I'm dying to give Gabriel his New Year's present.

He has no idea what it is. It's a sword. I bought it from a store in Chinatown that specializes in martial arts. The sword is beautiful. Complete with Sword, sheath, tassel, and box, it is meant for Tai Chi.

Early on in my son's life, he and I used to have pretend sword fights. When I give it to him, I will try to jog his memory of this. He and I would come charging at each other, with plastic swords in hand, and one of us would collapse to the floor, and play dead, only to stand back up and start again. It was fun.

Prize of all prizes, a CD album has recently found its way into my collection of recorded music. On Friday morning, I went to HMV on

Robson. At 10:00am, I was the first one through that door. It was David Bowie's sixty-ninth birthday, and his new record was being released.

Reaching the first shelf, I saw it. The twenty-fifth studio album by the god of rock and roll. *Blackstar.* But, I didn't stop there. No, I continued towards the shelf where all of Bowie's other albums were kept, and selected my four favourite ones.

On the bus ride back home, I heard a voice saying *Sold! Another Gold Record!* It seemed to be my father's voice, and he seemed to be watching me as though by way of surveillance, commenting on what I was doing. It was nothing new. In fact, while I was experiencing the auditory hallucination, I reflected on how boring and repetitive my voices are.

Peace be with the entities behind the voices I hear. I don't wish anything bad on anyone. If there's any grain of truth to be found in my delusions, I just want the people who are watching me, monitoring me, persecuting me, to go in peace and leave me alone.

Have mercy!

Eventually, in my artistic career, however far into the future, I would like to see my fifty-five books (under the title 'Father Son') available in e-book formats, and also printed and bound in ten volumes. This will be completed under 'Bryn Genelle Ditmars' (my author name). But, as for the two or three thousand hours of audio recordings and the two or three thousand works of visual art, these projects will be under 'Asananda' (my artist name).

Coming back to the memories at hand, I got off the bus, and started walking in the direction of my apartment building. Another voice: *Gold record! Another one! He makes it look so easy! We'll see what he thinks of the CD...*

I opened the front door, and reached for my key to check the mail. Then, I walked upstairs to the second floor and unlocked the door to my apartment. Immediately, I went straight for the stereo, and pressed play.

Each and every one of the seven songs resonated with me deeply. Listening, I took a moment to reflect upon my vicarious relationship with the famous rockstar, never having actually met him. I recalled my high school years, when I had a lingering suspicion that I was his father or I was his son, come from the future to reincarnate as nothing more than one of his billion or so obsessed fans.

Suddenly, I heard a lyric in one of the songs. I could have sworn that I had written it or recorded it on my tape recorder years ago. I wondered if Bowie had stolen it from me, just in order to test me to see if I was nuts enough to recognize it and claim it as my own. But, I just sat there, at my coffee table, puffing on my nicotine vaporizer, listening.

Old and out of fashion were the voices I was hearing. *Would you look at that. Bryn's a giga-billionaire! Amazing. Look, Bryn. You may very well be the wealthiest man on the planet, but you have to make it first. Make it your own! It's gotta come from you!*

For a brief moment there, I was interpreting the voice of my father as a reality. I puffed once more on my vaporizer, and went into the kitchen to make lunch. I knew that what the voices were saying wasn't true. I knew I wasn't a 'giga-billionaire'. I knew I had a hundred bucks to my name. In fact, I felt like talking back to thin air, correcting the voice and pointing out just how inaccurate the label was. The voice left me panic-stricken. But, it was nothing I wasn't used to.

Zion, in my epic poetic mythology, is the feminine personification of the emanation of the New Jerusalem. Her masculine counterpart is 'X'. Zion and X are the father and mother of Asananda and Xavier. I have written millions of words surrounding this mythological lineage. And, this is where my insanity and my imagination overlap.

I met with my two best friends the next day, at the cafe. The Quiet One and The King Of Chronic Insomnia were there to meet me, at our favourite table near the back. It was his turn to pay for the coffee. So, I waited patiently for my drink to arrive. Then, the miraculous conversation began. We talked for three hours.

On our way out the door afterwards, however, I was starting to have mild symptoms. I took a PRN and continued walking westbound. The King Of Chronic Insomnia and I said goodbye to The Quiet One, and went to a Japanese restaurant for sushi. As I sat there at the table I began to feel as though I was not myself, not Bryn, not Genelle, not Ditmars, but S.A. Of course, this abbreviation of my power name from the Golden Dawn does have a direct connection to my identity. But, it seemed like the voices were judging me.

Now, after dinner, I said goodbye to my friend, and continued on my way home. It was 6:30pm. Just enough time before meds and bed to listen to *Blackstar*. That was Saturday night. It is now Sunday morning. And, I am looking forward to seeing my clients this coming week. I'm doing peer support work and presentations to be of service to humanity. And, also, to keep me out of trouble!

PROPHET AND PROPHETESS
CHAPTER 17

FAR AS I CAN RECALL, RIGHT AROUND THE TIME I SAW THE BUMPER stickers that said *Repent Sinner*, there was another strange event. The Scarab and The Mad Scientist had set up an orientation with a man who was inquiring about the order.

One afternoon, I was just hanging out in the temple house, when the Hierophant and Hierus came walking towards me in the kitchen, saying they needed my help. They explained the situation to me, and asked if I could wait in the office for a man who wanted a few questions answered. I agreed, and did so gladly, happy to be of service.

Upon the man's punctual arrival at the front door, I let him in and showed him to a chair where he was to wait. He seemed like an ordinary fellow, and it was easy for me to imagine him being initiated into Neophyte, and becoming my frater. Soon enough, The Mad Scientist and The Scarab came walking down the hall, finished with whatever they were doing. From there, they took over, and led the man into the office.

Returning to the kitchen in the back, I boiled some water and made some herbal tea to drink. I turned on some music. Whatever my French-Canadian brothers and sisters were listening to. I think it was Nick Cave.

So, there I sat, passing the afternoon with a certain sense of dignified leisure and solace.

Eventually, the orientation was done. They came to join me in the back, laughing at something that eluded even my keenest sense of irony. I didn't have a clue as to what was so funny. So, I asked them to explain.

Quickly, The Mad Scientist disclosed the subject of their humour. Apparently, the strange man had showed them a manuscript he had written based on the laws of Thelema. The Scarab had immediately corrected the man, and made it very clear that the Golden Dawn did not teach or practice that sort of magic.

Unless he was mistaken, however, the man made it very clear that he had accurately interpreted a verse of poetry in one of Crowley's books. Evidently, Crowley had written a kind of prophetic prayer in which he predicted that a prophet and a prophetess were destined to arrive at a place called 'Hastings'. The man insisted that the famous black magician had actually meant Hastings, as in Main and Hastings, the closest intersection only a block and a half away from the temple house.

And, Crowley had written that a couple, man and wife, were going to appear before the adepts and conceive children. These children were said to be the ones to save the world. Now keeping in mind the fact that the man was crazy and eccentric in his convictions, I did not feel that The Scarab and The Mad Scientist were giving this incident enough symbolic credit. And, immediately, I thought of Sunflower and myself.

Like minded, she and I had achieved companionship for about a year and a half now. And, we were both very creative in our art forms. She was in Portal and I was in Philosophus, and we were priestly in our roles. But, our love relationship had since ended, and there were no children between us.

So, for the days that followed, I put it behind me for the most part. I continued to work at the commercial art studio, and continued teaching o=o every Monday, and continued attending the 4=7 class every Friday. Also, a big part of my life was taking place at my brother's place, a venue which I called The New Jerusalem. On his stage, I hosted a weekly night of spoken word every Sunday evening. But, very few people showed up to participate in the open mic, which I called The Spoken Logos.

Soon, Halloween came. And, I found a lovely young woman whom I liked a lot. It didn't help any to consider that she had given me a bite of a chocolate marijuana brownie when the party was just getting started. She and I fell in love that night, and I recited love poetry to her till the cows came home.

Elated so by the THC, I stayed awake, with her in my arms. And, I was kicking myself to think that I didn't write any of it down on paper. She and I laughed and laughed, and loved and loved some more. I called her Jerusalem.

Very soon after Halloween, she started contributing to my brother's rent. And, I visited her daily, and suggested that she join me at the tile factory. Until Christmas, she worked in the packing department, while I poured the plaster. On the last day of work before the Christmas holidays began, we both received a small cash bonus, and she was cordially relieved of her duties. But, I would return to work in January.

Envisioning a life together, Jerusalem and I grew very close. She came with me to Rainbow Lake for Christmas and New Year's. As a gift, my father presented me with a small micro-cassette recorder. That was the beginning of my addiction to recording thoughts, lines of poetry, ideas, conversations, and various notes to myself. At the stroke of midnight, somewhere between December 31st of 1999 and January 1st of 2000, we circled round a big bonfire, getting drunk on champagne.

None of my friends knew of my involvement in the order. They must have found it odd that I never invited them over to my place. But, my lips were sealed, all in order to ensure the integrity of the spiritual alembic that surrounded the temple house, even if it *was* near Main and Hastings. I rarely ever saw Sunflower, except on several occasions where I heard her crying out loud in the temple beside my bed. The walls were paper thin.

FROM GOD'S LIPS TO MY EAR
CHAPTER 18

TODAY, I WOKE UP AT 7:30 IN THE MORNING. I HEARD MY CELL PHONE go off. It was a text from Gabriel's Godfather, saying that David Bowie had died of cancer yesterday (two days after his sixty-ninth birthday). I couldn't believe it, and it hit me pretty hard.

His music was the reason why I had survived my teenage years. So, his death is a difficult pill for me to swallow. *And I'm really good at swallowing pills!* But, it's more than that. It's more than just a reminder of my own mortality. It's a wake up call that causes me to reflect on my life and the role that Bowie played in my experience.

Early yesterday, I made a list of things to do. Chores. And, each chore that I set out for myself was another reason why I was reluctant to visit my son. I had to take out the garbage, do the recycling, go to the bank, shop for groceries, and do the laundry. Generally, I was grumpy. So, it was the rebellious spirit in me that made me walk over to my mother's place and watch television, in the advent of the Golden Globes. I felt like going on strike from life. So, by the time the award show started and my mother got home, I announced that I hadn't taken out the garbage, I hadn't done the recycling, I hadn't gone to the bank, I hadn't shopped for groceries, and I hadn't done the laundry. And, I even had every impulse to relapse on cigarettes. Bowie used to smoke three packs a day.

So, waking up this morning to the horrific news, I realized that I didn't have any coffee, cream, fruit, cereal, or almond milk. Recovering robustly from yesterday's stubbornness, I thought *Bowie would want me to have a good breakfast.* And, I went to buy groceries. For him.

Home again, I called my mother, and she consoled me. She knows how much Bowie meant to me and millions of other people. Then, I checked Facebook, and saw what was trending, just to make sure it wasn't just a bad dream. Then, after breakfast, I went to work. While I was on the bus, The Princess Of Maybe Later (one of my ex-girlfriends) texted me saying she couldn't believe it. Then, while I was having coffee on Commercial Drive, Sunflower texted me, saying that she thought of me when she heard the news.

And, then I met my Monday morning client. The visit was good. Then, I had to go meet my Monday afternoon client. I received a call from him, saying that he had to cancel the appointment. Then, my uncle called me from Toronto, and left a message on my voicemail. Immediately, I caught the bus to my mother's house (taking advantage of her free long distance), and returned his call. He, of course, knew how much David Bowie had meant to me, and we talked.

David Bowie. David Bowie. David Bowie. He truly was a god.

Over five decades, he performed countless concerts, and recorded twenty-five studio albums, essentially changing the world of art forever. But, the way I remember it, and as I told my uncle, I first discovered his music when I was fourteen, when I was in grade eight at Ideal Mini School. Then, modelling my own fashion after him, I became a big fan, skateboarding around Vancouver with a neon green mohawk, plugged into my walkman listening to a tape of his first major album *Hunky Dory*.

Well over three years of teenage angst later, I discovered the god of rock and roll's more current work, right around the time I was introduced to marijuana. I remember saving up my baby-sitting money, and buying two tickets to the *Outside* tour in Tacoma, Washington. My sister made a deal with me. She was willing to rent a car and go there with me in exchange for the second ticket. It was a plan.

On the exterior, I was functional and rational, but on the inside I was under the impression that I was somehow genetically related to the icon. The concert was featuring him and Trent Reznor from Nine Inch Nails. It was a great concert. And, a first!

From then, I remember a high school buddy of mine inviting me to come see David Bowie in concert a second time. This time, it was in Vancouver, and I found myself standing less than twenty feet away from the rock idol. He was an hour late getting started. But, when he got there, he was there. The opening song, "Quicksand", started with an enigmatic lyric. *I'm closer to the golden dawn, immersed in Crowley's uniform of imagery.* About to be initiated into the aforementioned order, I too was closer to the golden dawn. I felt as though that song was being sung directly to me.

Then, in grade twelve, I bought a pair of baggy white coveralls, and applied acrylic paint to the fabric. On my left sleeve, I wrote the word 'anxiety', and on the right sleeve I painted the word 'descending'. And, on the back, I did my own rendition of Bowie's self portrait from the cover of *Outside*.

He and I shared the same initials. His were 'db' (Death Birth), and mine were 'bd', (Birth Death). I remember musing obsessively over the coincidental connection.

Eventually, my admiration for him became more mature and sincere. Almost spiritual. Little did I realize that years later, I was going to be hallucinating his voice and delusionally believing beyond a shadow of a doubt that he was watching me each and every hour of every day, commentating on my every word and every deed, who I was with, what I was saying, what I was doing, and where I was. I first hallucinated his voice back in 2001. And, the most recent hallucination of him commenting on my life was about five minutes ago.

Casting a backwards glance, I can honestly attest that I've been hearing his voice and the voice of Trent Reznor for longer than my thirteen year old son has been alive. Hard to believe. But, there you have it. Even early on in 2000, when I was living at the temple house in Gastown, I was dreaming of fame and fortune similar to his.

Radio was the very first format for my delusions of grandeur. In February of the final year of the twentieth century, I appeared on the air on the radio station out at the university, on a spoken word program called 'Hearsay'. I visited CITR studio at UBC twice, right around the time I was hosting 'The Spoken Logos' at The New Jerusalem. Once, I was a guest speaker, and once I hosted an hour long instalment while the regular programmer was away on holidays. My girlfriend at the time, the one I had met on Halloween of 1999, the one with whom I had welcomed in Y2K, the one who worked along side me at the tile factory, the one whom I truly loved (though not more than I loved my tape recorder), the one whom I had invited to come with me to Rainbow Lake, she dumped me on Valentine's Day of 2000.

On the last day of February and the first day of March, single again, I invited my film maker friend, The Earl, to collaborate on a documentary video. He agreed to my proposal. And, we used his Hi8 camera and microphone to document a ritual surrounding the shaving of my head. I had very long hair and a beard at the time, so the transformation was quite profound. I came from the East, I came from the West, I came from the South, I came from the North, and arrived at the doorstep of The New Jerusalem in the alley at Main and Hastings.

Stoically toying with the idea of being the reincarnation of Jesus Christ, I called the film 'The Making of The Last Messiah'. Intellectually, I didn't believe I was Christ, but the hookers in the alley did.

Sitting on the cold wet concrete at my feet, kneeling, a prostitute, high on heroin probably, held out her hands towards me, with eyes wide open, staring. *Are you for real? I don't believe it! It's you! Jesus Christ! Can I touch your hand?* Looking a lot like the stereotypical vision of the anointed one, I probably reminded a lot of people of the saviour. But, I just smiled and nodded. I had a film to shoot.

BEHOLDING A VISION IN WHITE
CHAPTER 19

THEN, IN EARLY MARCH OF 2000, I QUIT MY JOB AT THE STUDIO, I MADE a clean break from my girlfriend, I adopted my middle name, I shaved my head on camera, I moved out of Tehuti, and I prepared to leave Vancouver for the country again. But, before I left the city, I went to go visit The Lady By The River. I had been working with her for the past six months, at the tile factory, and had an enormous crush on her.

Her huge success as a creative artist was very inspiring to me. So, sharing my work with her, I brought along some samples of my calligraphy. I recorded our hourlong visit on my micro-cassette recorder, and we bid one another farewell.

Escaping, as it were, from urban life, I packed up all my books in boxes, and did my very best to prepare for yet another yearlong love affair with my muse of epic poetry. I knew full well that my old log cabin was waiting for me. I knew full well that Temple Calliope was still there, patiently anticipating my divine return to the woods. I knew I had it in me to create once more. So, I did.

Emerging from Thoth's long pointed beak, I transported my belongings to my mother's house near Granville Island, and gathered art supplies from Opus, art supplies that were going to prove useful for the task at hand.

Yes, it *was* a shock. Almost traumatic, leaving the temple house. In retrospect, I can honestly say that those otherworldly experiences which my life in the order entailed were the makings of my consequent mental and emotional trauma.

Each and every day for those past several months or so, I had entered and exited the sublime installation of our communal rendition of a full Solomonic temple. One minute, I was banishing, invoking, summoning, meditating, visualizing, vibrating, and contemplating the mysteries of the universe. And, the next minute, I was in the back alley of the poorest neighbourhood in Canada, smoking pot with Lotus Noesis, or performing poetry at a local open mic, stepping over needles with just sandals on my feet.

So, the term that comes to mind is 'Alternate World Syndrome' (AWS). It is a mental disorder of sorts, caused by repetitive and disruptive transitions between two or more very different, almost opposing, environments. I would go from the sacred temple environment to the profane street life environment every single day. Normally, AWS is the direct result of using virtual reality or a direct result of the trauma from which war veterans suffer. I believe that I should probably be diagnosed with this illness, due to the stark environmental contrast which I experienced daily from August of 1999 to March of 2000.

Oh yeah. I almost forgot. Before I returned to Rainbow Lake, I made an overnight sojourn to the Sunshine Coast, where my old friend, Car, was living. It was March 15th. I went to Horseshoe Bay, caught the ferry to Langdale, and hitch-hiked to her place in Robert's Creek, where there was a party going on. We ate magic mushrooms, and went out dancing that night, at the community hall.

From across the room, on the busy crowded dance floor, I saw a beautiful woman. She was dressed in white, with long flowing black hair. I couldn't take my eyes off her. I was stoned out of my mind, when she come dancing towards me where I sat. Little did I know that she would eventually end up being the mother of my child.

Embracing me, The Mother Of Gabriel smiled and flirted. I was speechless. How a woman so beautiful could be fond of a madman like me was beyond my understanding. I didn't know what to do. So, I invited her to come live with me in the forest for a year, while I wrote my epic poem. She smiled, and told me that she had to decline my invitation.

Not knowing how to react, I pulled out my micro-cassette recorder, and made a note to myself not to forget her. Ever.

Older than me, The Mother Of Gabriel never left my mind that night. Car and her friends and I crashed out on the floor of her two bedroom flat. The next day, I rolled a small joint, taking from the house supply of pot. I returned to Vancouver, the next day.

Come noon, I loaded up my stuff into the back of my mother's big blue station wagon, and we drove to Williams Lake, where I transferred all my belongings into my father's truck. Then, the morning after that, on Highway 20, heading West, my dad and I conversed. I told him everything about my life. And, he told me everything about his life.

He and I were very happy to see each other again. We arrived at the ranch just after sundown, on March 18th. I unpacked my books and clothes, and set up my desk, preparing for the composition of the poem that turned out to be my magnum opus.

A SIX-FINGERED HAND
CHAPTER 20

SO, BACK TO MY LIFE ON THE RANCH, I WOKE UP WITH THE RISING SUN on the morning of the first day of spring, ready with my pen and paper, ready to compose the rhyming couplets comprising what turned out to be my very best work. I would have had no hesitation keeping me from pouring out a plethora of blood, sweat, and tears. But, black ink was more effective, I decided.

I sat down at my desk in the eastern altar, afoot my handmade brass tripod, with fountain pen in hand, with my psychic aura open to the forces at work, dressed in my long white writing robe. My feline familiar was cuddled in my lap, purring contentedly. On top of the tripod, there was a white candle. Under the tripod, there was a small black basin of water, above which a white feather hovered magically.

Now, looking out the window, I could see the creek and the forest. The sky was partly blue and partly cloudy. I felt like I was in heaven. Then, my mind surprised me immensely. Up among the clouds, I visualized a giant hand reaching down to me. The hand had six fingers. At that precise moment, I came to the conclusion that it was the hand belonging to the archangel of the zodiac. The hand of Ratziel.

God was sending me a sign. The hand pointed to a small ring that was positioned abase the tripod. *The ring of Ratziel!* Of course, I took the auspicious sign to mean that I was meant to wear the ring on the smallest finger on my right hand, every minute of every hour that I wrote. So, I did.

Like any ordinary mystic, I was experiencing a vision. But, unlike any healthy sage, I was delving into the deepest depths of the boundless ocean of Samsara. Yet, it felt like Nirvana. I guess that's just the divine paradox that goes along with the territory. And, it was.

Elated, I wrote about Zion and X, as well as entities from over fifty of the world's mythologies. Gods and goddesses. Angels and archangels. Spirits and intelligences. Elemental kings and elementals. I wrote with a sense of pure passion, while wearing that small silver ring.

With my mind focussed entirely on the task of writing the epic, I minimized my mundane chores. I chopped kindling, because I needed to light a fire in order to heat my house. I hauled buckets of water from the creek, because I needed to drink herbal tea. I shovelled manure, because the garden needed to be fertilized. I made dinner, because I needed to be fed. I washed the dishes, because I well... You get the idea.

Heaven *does* exist. Of this, I was certain.

I wrote, and wrote, and wrote some more. Then, after the first four prophecies had been written, I arranged it so that I would fly to Denver, Colorado, with my mother, on a road trip down around the four corners in the states. We rented a car, and drove to Boulder, where we stayed for a couple days enjoying life as tourists. I had an orientation at Naropa, the buddhist university that had been founded in the early 70's. One night on Pearl street, I was introduced to The Troubadours of Divine Bliss, who were busking.

The journey brought my mother and I south to New Mexico, west to Arizona, north to Utah, and east back to Colorado. We even visited Zion national park. I was amused.

Eventually, after visiting the grand canyon and several other notable places, we returned the car to the car rental place, and caught a flight back to Vancouver. Then, I took the greyhound to Williams Lake, where I was picked up by my father. He and I returned to Anahim Lake, and then finally back to Rainbow Lake. I told him that the trip with my mother had been amazing, but that I was looking forward to getting back to writing.

My spring turned to summer turned to fall turned to winter. By February, I had written all the poetry, and was working on the calligraphy and illustrations, along with two title pages. When I wasn't working on my opus, I was writing a book of songs. One hundred songs. All of them were written in the month of February. On the 23rd, I turned 22.

And, that's when I got a call from my old friend, Cranked-and-Ready-to-go. He was inviting me to come with him on a road trip to California. His filmmaker friend, The Buddha, was also going, along with a few other artist types. I said that I was interested.

Like that, I was about to be shipped off to the states once more. Back in Vancouver, I realized the scoop. Cranked-and-Ready-to-go was broke. And, it was basically up to me to buy the bus tickets. Fortunately, I had managed to save some cash from the carpentry jobs I did. So, with another epic poem under my belt, I went from East Van to San Fran, with a big bushy beard on my face.

End of all ends, after touring our poems in the seediest bars and clubs, we managed to return to B.C. The Buddha mentioned to me that one of the rooms in his house was vacant. I grabbed the opportunity like lightning, and moved into that house near Commercial Drive. Little did I know that that house was going to be the house where I lost my mind.

BELIEF'S INTREPID SOLDIER
CHAPTER 21

THE COMMERCIAL ART STUDIO HIRED ME BACK ON, JUST AFTER I MOVED into the house. The Buddha was living in the small room next to mine. And, on the other side of my room, there was a beautiful, though very dyslexic, German waitress. In May of that year, I decided to shave my face. The Dyslexic German Waitress and I shared a few intimate massages. And, I was taking lots of photographs with my manual camera.

Holding it on top of a small tripod, I made use of the timer, and posed repeatedly in and around the house. It was spring. So, we thought we would have a garden party. We invited friends and family members to come plant flowers, herbs, vegetables, and various shrubs. I was really into getting my hands dirty in the soil.

Eventually, I was getting very busy with socializing, after twelve months in the wilderness. And, I think it was May 15th when I attended an event at the Vancouver East Cultural Centre. Car was there, as well. She gave me a small toke of a joint, before we both went inside to see the show.

Later that night, I was dancing ecstatically. I felt like I was the centre of everyone's attention. Then, as I left the building to go home, the future mother of Gabriel was waiting outside to say hello. I told her that

I remembered meeting her the previous year. So, I had no hesitation in inviting her over to my place for a cup of late night tea.

And, tea it was!

She spent the night with me. We fell in love. I told her all about my time up north. And, the next morning, we went for a walk down the street to her sister's place. I told her that falling in love is like remembering your dreams. She was so excited by that statement that she wrote it down on a sheet of paper in colourful pencil crayons.

Totally inspired by each other, we continued to share intimate moments. But, then, she had to leave on a plane to Nova Scotia, to visit one of her sisters. We spoke on the telephone several times while she was away. But, as much as I felt completely devoted to her, I was still very flirtatious with two or three other young women. It was overwhelming to be in a social environment, after a year in the bush. My feline familiar came to live with me. And, eventually, I got involved in the rave scene.

My pet cat saw less and less of me. Instead of curling up in my lap while I wrote, like it was at the ranch, she spent endless days alone in my room, coming in and out through the open window. Then, when my girlfriend returned to Vancouver, she started living with me. And, as spring turned to summer, I started spending my weekends at the Portal Space, with the members of a group called Tribal Harmonix. I smoked pot, and made tape recordings, and even tried MDMA once.

And, when I did, I was up all night dancing to the music that was being played by the DJ's. However, the very next morning, I had to go to work. I was very dehydrated, as a result of the hit of ecstasy that I had taken. My behaviour intensified.

Now, recording my life on tape, and taking photographic self-portraits with my manual camera, I was also keeping a journal. The journal entries got stranger and stranger, as time went by. I remember thinking I was very special and unique beyond my years. Delusions of grandeur were only a flicker of the eyelash away. And, not surprising, the sudden and drastic transition from country to city was proving to be slightly traumatic for me.

One fine sunny day in September, right around 9/11, Gabriel's Mother and I woke up and looked out the bedroom window into the garden. I noticed that, growing in the corner of the yard, by the fence, there was a seven foot marijuana plant. I harvested it, dried it, and started smoking it. Daily.

Now, I can honestly say that I still have tape cassettes that I recorded back in those days. And, many of them include arguments between Gabriel's Mother and me. She would scream at me, cursing and swearing violently, trying to discourage me from smoking pot. But, the more she persisted, the more I resisted. And, it was a vicious cycle, indeed. As weeks went by, I became very withdrawn and antisocial.

Early in autumn, on October 15th, Gabriel's Mother and I went to the Sunshine Coast. We had been invited to a house called Mountain Song, where an old witch lived. Two of our friends also lived in that house. One of them was passing out magic mushrooms. My girlfriend ate one, and I ate one. Suddenly, we were high.

And, voices clouded my mind. *He's the elfin king. And, she's the elfin queen! They are the ones we sent for! They will conceive a child! Forget Mary and Joseph! These two are elfin royalty!*

Relentlessly, and for the remainder of that evening, the two of us were tripping badly. We went to a dance party that night, where we moved in ways that were previously unimaginable. Then, back at her family's old and luxurious cabin on the beach, we went to sleep. The next day, having come down from the drug trip, we walked, arm in arm, along the shoreline, just east of Robert's Creek pier.

Then, my girlfriend told me that she wanted to have a baby. I told her that I could probably help out with making that happen. And, that very night, we conceived our son, Gabriel.

Her arms embraced mine. I was twenty-two. She was twenty-seven. We had visions of our future lives together. And, elfin royalty or not, we returned to Vancouver and the house near Commercial Drive. She believed in me, and I believed in her. I continued with my prolific art and writing. And, she did childcare for one of her mother's friends. I spent October, November, and December smoking marijuana every chance I got. The voices persisted. And, soon, I started to believe that there were cameras and microphones everywhere. I thought my life (the life of the messiah, no less) was being broadcast over the internet for all the world to see.

GIVING A VOICE
TO THE VOICELESS
CHAPTER 22

DOES IT EVER GET ANY BETTER THAN THIS? I MEAN, REALLY. I'M 95% cured of schizophrenia, with the help of heavy antipsychotic medications. And, as my psychiatrist said recently, I'm like Van Gogh, except I still have my ear! I'm living on disability, with my food, shelter, and clothing covered. I'm in a one bedroom apartment in mental health housing, the first legitimate housing situation I've ever had. I love my job as peer support worker, and enjoy volunteering as a public speaker. Also, last but not least, I am in a healthy relationship with everyone in my life. Things to be grateful for!

Residual schizophrenia is what I'm battling. But, with a community of devoted people in my life, I'm happy. Like just yesterday… I went to meet with one of my peer support work supervisors. We had a great discussion, and I handed in my monthly activity log. Then, I arrived at the Waves coffee house for a second meeting. This time, it was on the topic of arranging logistics for nomination. Two of my colleagues from BCSS were there to meet with me, showing their determination to nominate me for the Courage To Come Back award.

Elated, and honoured, I sat down with the provincial co-ordinator, to go over details regarding the application form. The Quiet One was also there, with a copy of last year's details. Then, a family member of someone with schizophrenia arrived.

And, for the next hour, we brainstormed ideas to include in the nomination process. I was right there, ready to answer and give further details about my struggles and accomplishments. Far from mute. However, at 3:30, after talking and taking notes, we had to conclude.

My third meeting of the day began when my good friend, The King Of Chronic Insomnia, arrived. As soon as I said goodbye to my colleagues, I said hello to him. We found a table, and started our weekly visit. I told him that The Quiet One was going to be there in a few minutes. But, I was in need of nicotine, and didn't have the wherewithal to go outside for a quick puff. He asked me several questions. I was unable to offer more than one word responses. I was experiencing what my doctor calls 'thought-blockages'. And, the result was temporary mutism.

When The Quiet One returned, I bought coffee for all of us. I was struggling to make sense of what was going on. Voices emerged into my awareness: *He's buying coffee! But, he forgot to have lunch! The most important man alive is down to his last five bucks! To hell with him! He is sitting on a goldmine of unpublished manuscripts! Who are they? The ones he's with must be evil! He's definitely schizophrenic! He could be the one! Yes, we're sure. It's been established. Watch and wait!*

Eventually, after listening to the conversation, I thought it would be best for me to go outside for a few puffs of vapour. That stabilized me fairly effectively. I finished my coffee, and reached my hand into my pocket, pulling out an orally dissolving tablet of olanzapine. I placed it on my tongue. And, miraculously, within ten minutes, I was finally able to contribute something to the three-way conversation.

And, I was fixated on the small glints of light in the eyes of my two best friends. The points of light were distracting in the moment. But, I managed to see past these distracting hallucinations. We talked from 3:30 to 6:30. Another wonderful visit.

Voicing our thoughts, we concluded by getting up and going outside onto the rainy streets. Right away, The King Of Chronic Insomnia ran into one of his clients, on the sidewalk, leaving The Quiet One and myself to briefly chat. I apologized for my mutism earlier. She said that I didn't need to apologize. So, I took it upon myself to apologize for apologizing.

Emerging back into the cold and wet January weather, we started walking westward. At the corner of Broadway and Oak, I said goodbye to both of them, and continued walking down to my apartment building. As soon as I got inside and settled, I made some rice and vegetables, and listened to more of Bowie's music.

Reflecting on my life, I glanced over to a small framed picture of my thirteen year old son, Gabriel. I took my nightly meds, and went to bed, after plugging in my vaporizer battery to charge overnight. This morning, I awoke at 8:00am, and went to Granville Island for coffee with my mother. We talked, and she sent me home with a bag full of food.

SMOKING MYSELF SIMPLE
CHAPTER 23

THE FALL OF 2001, I SPENT MY DAYS, ROLLING JOINT AFTER JOINT, scribbling in my incoherent journal, and making tape upon tape, documenting my life, which I thought was the life of the messiah. So, it made perfect sense to me that the cassettes were worth millions of dollars a piece, being sold at private auctions to people like Madonna and David Bowie and Bono from U2.

Having been laid off from the tile factory, I was free to pass the time taking pictures and doing whatever I wanted to do in terms of artistic projects. I was chain-smoking hand-rolled cigarettes of yarrow, kinnickinick, mullein, sage, and marijuana. My poor girlfriend was worrying about me, yelling at me as way of warning. She wholeheartedly discouraged me from smoking. But, I carried on, in spite of her telling me not to.

Each day that passed, my friends fell to the wayside. I spent more and more time in my room, treating it as a stage of sorts. I was particularly suspicious of the chandelier, which I believed had hidden microphones and cameras. Taking self-portraits on colour film, black and white film, and slide film, I wandered through the house, capturing my hellish dungeon existence.

Come Christmastime, I had a substantial amount of THC running through my blood. I believed that the community should have been paying my rent. I was broke, living on handmade chocolate and oranges, because that was what I thought prodigies ate.

He's the prodigy of human nature! Look at him! He doesn't have any idea how prodigious he's being! The divine white scribe! He's the anointed one, without a doubt! But, he hasn't paid the rent! But, on the other hand, he's a giga-billionaire! Bowie loves the guy! Let's keep the film rolling! This is priceless!

And, so the voices went. Twenty-four hours a day.

Landing in the Nicola Valley right around the winter solstice, my girlfriend and I went to celebrate the holiday season with her family. It was Christmas, and I thought I was Christ. She was ten weeks pregnant. I was just a raver and a creative dilettante. The weight of the world was on my shoulders, and I began thinking that I was part of an alien cloning experiment. But, when in doubt, I took pictures. Picture after picture of my future family in law celebrating Christmas together.

Done with the festivities, my pregnant girlfriend and I returned to Vancouver and the house near Commercial Drive. Then, after new year's day, I smoked the last few leaves of marijuana, and resumed my industrious life as an artist who was behind on his rent.

Eureka! The man's amazing! He's a living icon! A real male grace! A male genius!

And, so the voices went. I received a lot of praise from the voices. And, I also received a lot of criticism from them too. None-the-less, I started to get used to the idea that I was being monitored. In my mind, I was world famous. Though, when I went to go buy groceries on Commercial Drive, the strangers I passed on the sidewalk pretended not to know me at all. So, I thought that people were deceiving me. But, I knew I was famous. The fame seemed like it was on an underground version of the internet: *The dark web.*

Not one to judge the voices, I believed everything they said, because I thought the people behind the voices were powerful and authoritative celebrities. I had visions of Bono from U2 sitting in his bathrobe smoking a cigar. I even had delusions about the people who lived in the house. The Buddha had moved out, along with The Dyslexic German

Waitress. Gabriel's Godfather had moved in, along with a young woman who worked at a snowboard factory. I thought that the lesbians upstairs were vampires. And, I vaguely recall hallucinating visions of a ghostly girl playing an upright piano where my writing desk was.

One night, it snowed. I woke up, looked outside my bedroom window, and saw the garden covered with white. I finished writing my journal, and went to work on consolidating my tape collection. Gabriel's Mother, who was showing a slight bulge in her belly, even helped me with making small cut-and-paste collages for the covers.

Realistically, I didn't know who I was. I didn't know what I was doing. I didn't know the world or where I belonged therein. I just had an overwhelming propensity to create. My feline familiar got a bad case of fleas. And, my girlfriend and I argued a lot.

And, then the strangest thing happened. Gabriel's Mother and Gabriel's Godfather were in the kitchen, talking. Of course, I thought that they were talking about me. And, I was bombarded with an enormous sense of paranoia and bewildering jealousy. I felt like I was about to explode.

Christ or not, I screamed at the top of my resinous lungs, jumped up into the air, and fell down heavy on the middle of my bedroom floor. Apparently, one of the neighbours called the police, and an officer arrived at the front door to see what the matter was.

Lying on the floor, I was crying, in tears, afraid that the world was ending because of me. The police officer came in, and determined that I was not a danger to myself or others, and left. If only the neighbour had called the ambulance instead, I might have been brought to the psyche ward and received a proper mental assessment. But, no.

Eventually, I was evicted. And, my girlfriend and I went to live with my mother near Granville Island. On the day of the big move, my father was there to counsel me. I walked from Commercial Drive to Granville Island, with the last of my things, and came stomping in through my mother's front door, on my way downstairs. My mother told me that I was not the messiah. I was confused. So, I went downstairs, and pulled a blanket over my head, hoping it would all just go away.

So, a month or so later, leading up to Easter, I was mute for several weeks. My mother brought me to see a psychologist. And, my girlfriend printed off something from the internet about 'schizoid personality disorder'. And, eventually, they took me to see a psychiatrist out at UBC hospital. Something was up. And, everyone in my life knew that something was definitely up. Everyone but me.

CARPENTERS HARD AT WORK
CHAPTER 24

TAKING IT DAY BY DAY, MY FRIENDS, MY FAMILY, AND I PRETTY MUCH carried on as usual, in spite of my bizarre behaviour. I recall a time when I was having an argument with Gabriel's Mother, in one of the bedrooms in the basement of my mother's apartment. I went into a full-blown fit, and screamed as loud as I could, and flopped myself down upon the bed, yelling into the pillows.

How it happened, I don't know. But, early that spring, sometime in April of 2002, my girlfriend was very pregnant, and somehow I managed to agree to a small building project. My father volunteered to help me put the second storey on a house that was already half built. That house was situated near the gate of the ranch belonging to my parents-in-law, and was called simply 'the gatehouse', oddly enough.

Early one morning, my father and I set out to work on the gatehouse. The carpenter and the carpenter's helper, at it again. Only, this time, the experience was very different. I was psychotic. I was hearing the voice of David Bowie and Trent Reznor: *It's Jesus! The carpenter! King of the jews! Look at him with his dad's pressurized nail-gun! He knows how to use it! Jesus Christ! The one messiah! It's true! We're certain it's him!*

So, the voices went, commenting on what I was doing. I struggled with putting each and every nail into wood, but by the end of the second day of work my father and I had successfully erected all the walls. I braced the walls, using diagonal posts, and put a bunch of nails to hold the walls in place. But, a big windstorm developed.

Overnight, huge gusts of wind came howling down the valley, and knocked down all the walls. In the morning, my father and I realized what we had done. I had put two-inch nails in, when I should have used three-inch nails. Meanwhile, I was engaging my father in pseudo philosophical conversation. We tried our best to salvage what remained of the walls. Piece by piece, we put it back up.

Now, late that afternoon, still hearing voices, I was climbing the aluminum ladder when I missed a step and fell. I collapsed on the ground, and hit my head on a pile of 2x4's. My father suggested that we call it a day. So, we went back to the barn-house for supper. I was mostly mute, and recording everything on my tape recorder. After we all had our evening meal, I was doing the dishes in a daze.

God! God's doing the dishes! Those tapes he's been making are worth millions! Can you imagine? The life of God on tape! He's gonna be a multimillionaire!

On that particular night, my mother-in-law had a bit of an altercation with me in the kitchen in the kitchen, while I scrubbed the pots and pans. She got mad at me for not talking, and she got mad at me for talking. My autistic tendencies made this very confusing to me.

From the kitchen, I ran. I ran across the ranch. I hopped the neighbour's fence, and ran straight up the hill. I ran beneath the full moon. I ran to get away. I ran to find myself. I left them all behind me, and I ran.

Singing under the bright full moon, I danced as though the whole world was watching. But, the whole world was *not* watching me. No one was.

On my way back down the hill, I heard a wolf howl from the forest nearby. I was still in bare feet, and the grass and rocks were hurting me. So, I returned to the house, and walked through the sliding glass door. Ignoring everyone there, I stomped on up the stairs, and hid in the attic. Then, I knelt down on the floor by the window, and started screaming at the top of my lungs.

Longing to be rid of this chronic paranoia, I was scared. It frightened me to think that I was part of an alien cloning experiment. It angered me that no one cared about me or my art. I was very afraid that my girlfriend and her family were extraterrestrial vampires from another dimension. I continued screaming.

Out of nowhere, my father entered the attic, and ordered me to be quiet. He yelled at me. But, I continued rocking back and forth on my hands and knees, screaming. Then, he grabbed my hair, and tried to drag me out. But, seeing I was not responding to the pain, he gave up. Then, my mother-in-law started yelling at me, saying that I was never going to be allowed to see my son. She, too, also gave up. But, the one good thing that came out of all this was that someone had the decency to call the ambulance.

My first gut reaction when the paramedics arrived was interesting. As soon as they took ahold of my arms and legs, I suddenly felt *safe*. As they carried me downstairs, my eyes were closed, my screaming stopped, and my limbs were completely relaxed. And, by the time they got me into the ambulance, I had retreated from the world into a state of catatonia.

Over the midnight moonlit landscape, I went. When we arrived at Kamloops general hospital, I was not responding to pain. They placed my lifeless body into a bed. My eyes were closed, but I could hear the moans and groans of the other patients on the psych ward. I thought the other patients were holographic projections of my alter-egos. I could hear the nurses, coming with their tap-tap-tapping footsteps up and down the hallways. But, I thought the nurses were aliens, conspiring with one another to program my mind.

Now, the room I was in felt safe. But, I was on a different planet, so to speak. Deep in catatonia, I reflected on my past few years. *Was I still in the order of the Golden Dawn? Did they let me fall away, because I didn't pay my annual dues?* I suddenly realized that I had been neglecting my daily rituals, and had broken my vows left, right, and centre. So, I got up out of bed, after thirty-six hours of catatonia, stood up, opened my eyes, and preformed the Cabalistic Cross, vibrating: *Ah-Tah! Malkuth! Vee-Geburah! Vee-Gidulah! Lay-Olam! Amen!*

DREAMING OF CIGARETTES
CHAPTER 25

MY MAIN AFFLICTION, IN TERMS OF SUBSTANCE USE, CAN BEST BE SUM-marized as an addiction to nicotine. I guess it could be worse and it could be better. Now, I recall one of my peer support work training program classes, when a doctor came to talk to me and my colleagues. He presented us with a surprising statistic: 89% of people suffering from schizophrenia smoke tobacco.

And, he pointed out that recent research has shown that there is a good reason for this. Apparently, nicotine is therapeutic in treating psychosis, acting as a sort of mood stabilizer. So, when a schizophrenic individual smokes, it is a form of self-medicating similar to marijuana or alcohol. However, the doctor went on to mention that the 'smoke' part of the cigarette experience is still very harmful.

Now, just the other day, after two and a half years of using my nicotine vaporizer, I broke down and bought a pack of really good quality cigarettes. Over the past two decades, I have gone through phases of smoking and non-smoking, but this is the first time I've ever considered it to be a 'relapse'.

Reflecting on this, I'd like to look at the big picture. Many if not most schizophrenics in Canada are living on disability social assistance. And, if nine out of ten of us smoke heavily, and considering that cigarettes are so expensive, it is safe to assume that a large portion of the monthly cheques go directly towards funding smoking habits.

And, where does that money come from? Tax dollars. For the past few years, I have been earning some money. But, I couldn't have been able to afford my vaporizer habit were it not for the money I've received from the provincial government.

Yes, for yesterday and today, I've been smoking cigarettes. Not heavily, but a substantial amount. And, yesterday afternoon, I met with my two best friends, The King Of Chronic Insomnia and The Quiet One, for our weekly coffee visit, at a local cafe.

Reclining back down in the comfortable chairs at the back, we sipped our espresso. Then, the funniest thing happened. The Quiet One reached into her bag, and procured a small plastic package. The package was full of individually wrapped fortune cookies. The cookies themselves were very old and stale. But, the fortunes were absolutely priceless.

Each of us took a turn at reading the fortunes hidden inside. The Quiet One read hers, and The King Of Chronic Insomnia read his. And, then it was my turn. Only, I had two. So, I read both of mine.

Very funny it was. The first one read: *Do not rush through life, pause and enjoy it.* But, then the second one said something a little bit contradictory: *Stop waiting! Buy that ticket, and take a trip today!*

I laughed so hard I almost choked on my coffee. We all laughed. Then, I went outside to have a cigarette. Still smiling silently to myself, I stood on the sidewalk, reached into my jacket pocket, pulled out a king sized regular North Fields, and lit it with my blue bic lighter.

Silently standing on the sidewalk, I inhaled the smoke, watching the traffic go back and forth along Broadway. When a big bus went barreling by less than two feet from where I stood, I remembered an incident from years ago. I had been riding the 22 through downtown, when there was some commotion on the street. A middle aged man with an overgrown beard and rags for clothes was trying to throw himself under the wheels of the moving bus. I was on the back of the bus, right by the window, so I saw it all.

Every single day since then, I thank my lucky stars that I'm not suicidal. That man must have been in a lot of pain. I hope he got the professional help that he needed. I think back to my mother's cousin, who killed himself because the pain of schizophrenia was too much.

Dropping my smouldering butt down into the gutter, I stepped on it, and the filter extinguished. I took one more long look at the traffic, and went back inside to reconvene with my two best friends, grateful to be alive.

FROM BEING GOD
TO PLAYING PING-PONG
CHAPTER 26

GOD WAS SPEAKING TO ME, OR SO IT SEEMED. BUT, AFTER ONE OF THE senior nurses had whispered into my ear, telling me that if I lay there for too long I'd get a blood clot and that I would be wise to get up out of bed, I came out of catatonia and performed the ritual which I had learned in the Golden Dawn. It must have been about 3:00am, when I stood up and made the motions of the Cabalistic Cross. Then, I went to the bathroom and emptied my bladder.

Right away, I approached the front desk, and did what just about every psych patient does when returning to sense: I asked the person behind the desk when I could leave. To my sincere disappointment, they informed me that I had been 'committed' and did not have permission to leave. It was my first feeling of imprisonment. I returned to my bed.

And, the following day, I returned to a semi-catatonic state. With my eyes closed, I was still very present. But, my girlfriend struggled to feed me. The voices were saying things like: *Look! They're trying to feed him! If he eats anything, that means he's gay! Look! He's eating! God is gay! Would you look at that!*

107

Coming to my senses took some time. The next day, I got a visitor. His name was Doctor S. I couldn't see him, because my eyes were still closed. But, I heard his voice when he said that he had been talking with my friends and family and had determined that I had been psychotic for more than six months. He told me that he was prepared to give me the diagnosis of paranoid schizophrenia, and that I would need to take anti-psychotic medication every day for the rest of my life. I cried, with my girlfriend by my side.

Enigmatically, Doctor S *gave* me the diagnosis, as though he was *giving* me some sort of gift. Almost out of generosity. Immediately, I thought to myself: *Thanks but no thanks, Doc! You can keep your damned diagnosis! I'm not taking any pills!* I was in denial, at first. But, then he told me that I would be restrained and injected if I refused to swallow the pill he was prescribing. In tears, I took the pill. One milligram of respirdone. Every night at bedtime.

Prescriptions are all a matter of random trial and error. Everyone responds differently. For me, it worked wonders. Within twenty-four hours, I was no longer thinking the nurses were aliens. And, interestingly, I remember feeling like I was sixteen again. But, then reality took hold, and everyone I spoke to reminded me that I was actually twenty-three. I grappled with the realization that my girlfriend was seven months pregnant. But, I managed to gather some courage and to do whatever it took to get out of the psych ward. During the interview with the doctor, I had scribbled a bunch of words onto paper. I read them back to myself. Suddenly, it hit me. I was *not* the messiah. I was a mental patient.

Reluctantly, at bedtime, I took another pill. And, as the days progressed, I was allowed out of the isolation unit and into the general psych ward, where individual beds were sectioned off by curtains. I signed up for an occupational therapy class, where we made ballon sculptures with paper and glue. I thought to myself: *This is a breeze! I kinda like not being the messiah! I'll make this dinky sculpture, and they'll let me out of here.* Also, there was ping-pong. What a strange activity! After years of delusion, I was finally 'normal'.

Only, just because I could play a game of ping-pong with my dad in the activity room, and not go into full-blown hysterics, this didn't make me 'normal'. The voices continued, growing only slightly fainter with the aid of medication. But, after eight long days of being in the hospital, and after countless games of ping-pong, they discharged me from Kamloops hospital.

Definitely looking at things with new eyes, I was sent to Vancouver to live with my mother. And, I started going to see a psychiatrist every week, at Kitsilano Fairview Mental Health Team. Doctor W agreed to take on my case. And, as soon as he saw that I thought my girlfriend was a vampire and that I was world famous, he urged me to go on disability right away. So, as told, I tried to avoid stress, while my girlfriend looked for a place for us to live.

I wasn't sane enough to work, but I was sane enough to realize that my girlfriend was nesting. And, as fortune would have it, she found us the perfect one bedroom suite on the top floor of a house nearby. It was within walking distance of both my mother's house and my mental health team. Hallelujah.

Giving it all I had, I persevered. I agreed to counselling, and took my meds. All my life, I had avoided taking pharmaceuticals, other than the occasional Tylenol tablet for the odd headache. It was new to me. And, though they told me that schizophrenia has no cure, I was determined to cure myself.

Yes, I was complying to meds, but in the back of my mind I was already making plans to try alternative approaches. But, first thing was first. My girlfriend, eight months pregnant, and I moved into our new place on July 1st, Canada Day, 2002. The window in the living room looked out into the leaves of a giant maple tree. Thoughts were going through my head at warp speed, making puzzles out of things. I contemplated the name of our glorious country, in the form of a question: *Can-a-da? (As in 'is a father able?')* My answer was: *Yes!*

AN ADDICTION TO FAILURE
CHAPTER 27

FROM THEN ON, THE FOCUS WAS MAINLY ON SUSTAINING A CERTAIN state of mental stability. But, also on the horizon was the inevitability of fatherhood. I took my pills, I rested, I slept like a log, I ate good food, and I began the momentous task of editing my books. The only computer that I had access to was at my mother's house, which was about a fifteen minute walk from where we lived. My girlfriend, now better regarded as my 'wife', was about to pop any day now.

I recall the night before Gabriel was born. Around 10:00pm, on July 17th, my wife and I went to bed. My wife asked me if I liked 'Gabriel' as a name. I told her I did, but that we were going to have to change the cat's name once the baby was born. I had taken my meds, so falling asleep was easy for me, even though sharing a bed with a pregnant woman is a bit like sleeping with a bowling ball. None-the-less, I managed to drift off to the realm of dreams.

Regardless, my sleep was disturbed around 1:00am. My wife was breathing very loudly. I opened my eyes, and asked her why she was breathing heavily. Then, I experienced a sudden serge of primal energy, realizing that it was time. So, I shot up out of bed, and volunteered to call the midwife. Then, about twenty minutes later, after I made sure my wife felt safe and comfortable, the midwife arrived.

Soon, my wife was moaning and groaning on the bed. The eastern skies outside were slowly growing brighter. She was trying to get comfortable, trying every physical position possible. Then, when she was ready to push, I had my arm around her shoulders on the bed. Then, the midwife announced that the baby's head was crowning. I touched Gabriel's forehead with my index finger.

The next thing I remember, my hand-held Sony tape recorder was recording our child's first cries. I felt so amazed by that sound. It was a healthy cry, and we all could tell that the baby was strong. There in the bedroom, up among the towering maple trees, at exactly 8:30am, on July 18th, 2002, my wife became a mother and I became a father. The feeling I had is impossible to describe. It felt a bit like butterflies in my stomach, and a bit like an ecstatic orgasm. All I could do was smile from ear to ear, and bless my lucky stars.

Precisely on time, the doorbell rang. I didn't have the faintest idea who it could be, so I ran downstairs to see who it was. Lo and behold! It was the diaper man, with a week's supply of cloth diapers. He was oriental, with a heavy accent, so it was difficult to hear what he was trying to say. But, I brought him upstairs, and he taught me how to properly fold the diapers. With only two hours sleep, I was pretty groggy. But, I thanked him for delivering the goods. Honestly, he couldn't have been more punctual if he had tried. Right on schedule!

Eventually, that day proved itself to be the very happiest day of my life. Gabriel, the baby boy, was born. And, Gabriel, the cat, adopted the name of 'Galadriel'. It was a lot to adjust to, but we all managed. Soon, the word got around that the birth was successful. My mother was first on the scene. She came, bearing food, which she put in the fridge and cupboards. Then, one after another, every day, for about a week or so, people arrived to pay homage.

Reflecting on this time in my life always gets me a bit teary-eyed. I am forever thankful for the fact that I was sober and sane enough to be present at my son's birth. My wife and I didn't leave the house at all for the first ten days. Everything that we needed was brought to us. Including cheesecake!

Soon, on a bright sunny day near the end of July, the three of us went for a long walk to Kitsilano beach, mother, father, and baby. We were careful to keep his eyes shaded from the sunlight. But, we managed. The days turned to weeks turned to months. And, before we knew it, we were full blown model of a nuclear family. Sort of.

Or, not. You see, soon after Gabriel was born, I surrendered to a sudden compulsion to buy a pipe and some tobacco, and start smoking again. The pattern in my life is all too reminiscent of failure. What did I do when I impregnated a woman? I developed schizophrenia. What did I do when the child was born? I went back to smoking tobacco. My list of behavioural relapses is a long one. However, it has been proven that schizophrenia is not due to a failure on the part of the individual. It's a flaw in chemistry, not a flaw in character. But, I didn't know this at the time.

Now, on the plus side of things, I was attending my weekly psych appointments at the mental health team, I was taking my meds religiously, and I was receiving money from disability. But, I felt like I had failed everyone in my life. Especially, myself! Instead of staying home with my wife and kid, I went down to my mother's apartment and typed my manuscripts into the computer and smoked my pipe, hungry for the sudden rush of nicotine.

THE GUY UPSTAIRS
CHAPTER 28

HAVE MERCY! JUST LAST NIGHT, AS I WAS DRIFTING OFF TO SLEEP, THE guy upstairs was shouting the same old thing. Over and over again, occasionally stomping on the floor.

Early this morning, as well, I heard the Tourettes-inspired verbal assault probably directed at some imaginary character. It required a certain degree of discipline on my part, in order to not take it personally. In the past, and even up until the present moment, I have been plagued by various forms of a delusion of persecution, and sometimes it feels like the verbal assaults are directed at me.

Remembering that the guy upstairs is not God, and remembering that I am not the messiah, I try my best to ignore the 'voice' coming from the third floor. He's got his challenges. I've got mine. But, come to think of it, he looks a lot like how I would imagine God to look. Grey hair. Beard. A crazy look about him. Etcetera…

On another note, he's always got the radio blasting away. Sometimes, I am able to discern exactly what song is being played. For these past two weeks, there has been noticeably more David Bowie than usual. Sometimes, I even dance along to it, pacing the floor of my living room, and humming quietly to myself.

It's Sunday, January 24th. Another Sunday morning. And, I'm feeling fine, aside from the inherent embarrassment of having relapsed on cigarettes again. But, I refuse to smoke inside my apartment. My preference is to take a walk around the block, while puffing. It's 8:41am. And, I've already smoked one.

Now, I'm just waiting for a text from my mother, who wants to go for coffee at Granville Island. Just not too early. She likes to sleep in. And, I respect that. There's nothing more demanding than the responsibility that comes along with being a midwife. Her sleep schedule is all over the place. Often, when she's on call, she works all night. The most recent time I asked her about how much sleep she had gotten, she was counting the minutes.

Each and every day that I live here in this mental health housing facility, I am torn. On the one hand, I feel overwhelmingly grateful that I have a roof over my head. And, on the other hand, it's depressing. But, regardless, according to the building manager, I will be moving out soon. After the guy upstairs leaves, I'm probably the next in line. They say I will be transferring over to what's called the SIL (semi independent living) program. I will be assigned a SIL worker, who will oversee my case. I have liked living here, but I am also excited at the thought of moving out. My heart goes out to God, and to the guy upstairs!

WHEN HUSBANDS ARE BANNED FROM THE HOUSE
CHAPTER 29

FOR THE REST OF MY LIFE, I WILL REMEMBER THE EXPERIENCE OF becoming a father. But, it's not an event, it's a process. And, it's not an achievement, but rather, a timeless transformation. In fact, here in early 2016, I am still learning the full implications of what it means to be called 'dad'.

Overcome with bliss on the day that Gabriel was born, and laughing out loud when I first saw him smile, I learned very quickly that my dear son had a great sense of humour. And, he still does. But, the first year of his life was full of ups and downs. I was adapting to my mental health diagnosis, and found myself torn between puffing on my tobacco pipe and changing diapers.

On the plus, I was being proactive with my treatment. In desperate search of alternative healing systems, I pursued a cure religiously. But, that got me into trouble. You see, in search of curative treatment modalities, I was researching like mad. While still under the care of Doctor W, and while still complying to therapy and pharmaceutical treatment, I regressed into psychosis several times.

Like the autistic prodigy that my voices told me that I was, I remember storming into the house one day, yelling and screaming. My wife and child escaped to the downstairs tenants right away, and were safe from the violence. I proceeded to trash the apartment, knocking over the television, throwing pillows off the couch, taking down decorations, and emptying the kitchen pantry, bag by bag, tossing the bulk of it all over the dining room floor.

See?! He's a real male prodigy! Look at him! He's throwing an hysterical fit! Obviously autistic! I agree! He's a danger to himself and a danger to others! Jesus Christ! The voices were incessant in those days. But, soon, Doctor W changed my meds from 2 milligrams of respirdone (which was causing me excessive fatigue) to 20 milligrams of olanzapine (which he suspected might be better).

Concurrently, I was using tobacco regularly and spending extensive time editing my manuscripts. And, repeatedly, my wife and I would have irrational arguments, and I was repeatedly ordered to leave. Variations of this happened a number of times. I felt so very frustrated. With my own wife against me, I really didn't have a clear sense of where I belonged.

And, one day, she accompanied me to the mental health team, as my advocate surprisingly enough. As soon as I walk into Doctor W's office, I started reading the first few pages of my earliest journals. He told me to stop. But, I was unresponsive. Then, the ambulance was called, and they took me away on a stretcher. I had my face buried in the pillow. And, as the paramedics brought me into the elevator, I reached my right hand in the general direction of my psychiatrist, and extended my middle finger.

Perhaps, I was angry. Angry at the world. Angry that no one gave me any recognition for my talent. Was I an internally tortured creative genius? Maybe. Did I deserve accolades for my gifts of artistic self-expression? Absolutely. Or so I thought. I was mad, in the most literal sense of the word. Mad to live. Mad to die. Mad to be stationed so deep in the lukewarm stewing-broth of compulsive denial. I didn't know what was going on. I insisted that I was the messiah. But, poor Doctor W recognized me as no such thing. Not even close!

Rage was in my veins, for the entire duration of my second hospitalization. I thought that I deserved praise from each of all the seven billion citizens of planet Earth. But, all I got was goofy looking hospital pyjamas and an orange with my name written on it. The one saving grace of psych wards, as I soon discovered, was the fact that they usually had a piano or two kicking about. I tapped the keys, one by one, in a clueless way. But, it was how I passed the day.

After I was discharged, I was sent to live with my mother again. It was devastating, to be so blatantly rejected by my own wife and son. But, I was in no state to care for such beautiful delicate beings. Then, I returned to live with them, eventually. And, then I was told to leave again. Then, I returned. I could hear voices of famous people, commenting on what I was doing. But, I was slowly developing some vague sense of insight.

God only knows how, but I was able to report, word for word, precisely what the voices were saying. The two people in my life who listened to me ramble on about it daily, were my mother and my wife. Bless them for listening. Making a verbal account of what the voices said was my own self-invented form of therapy. I was running by the seat of my pants, in those days!

Except, when I discovered Doctor A H, everything changed. Still on olanzapine, I went with my wife and our child to Victoria to meet the strange old wise octogenarian psychiatrist. It was an example of my determination to cure myself. He prescribed me several mega doses of vitamins and minerals, and encouraged me to eat food that was high in protein. Once we were back in Vancouver, I put my name on the waiting list to see a woman by the name of T W. She was one of only two ortho-molecular psychiatrists in the entire province of B.C.. She saw just how much I was in need of help, and took me on as one of her clients. Things were looking up.

THE PROFUNDITY OF SILENCE
CHAPTER 30

AND, I STILL HAD NOT TOLD ANYONE ABOUT MY INVOLVEMENT WITH the Golden Dawn. My parents didn't know, but they had their suspicions. My friends didn't know, but they might have guessed. My own wife had no idea as to the extensive history that I had with the order. I kept silent, for the most part, in fear of the threatened consequences alluded to in the vow that I took years previous. As far as my current involvement was concerned, I had fallen away almost entirely. The spring of 2001 was the last time that I had had any real contact with my brothers and sisters in the great work. I had notified my proctor that I was ready to graduate from Philosophus and advance into the grade of Portal. But, no one ever got back to me. So, that was how I left it.

Vast questions in the back of my mind were left unanswered. I was roaming lost in the wilderness, and I was in desperate need of spiritual guidance. By the fall of 2002, I was experiencing insanity, for lack of a better word. I believed my wife was an extraterrestrial vampire, I believed that I was the messiah, and I believed our son was an archangel. Almost compulsively, I would constantly fixate on numbers and letters: *Gabriel* (7 letters, meaning the angel of the moon) *Leonard* (7 letters, referring to the only zodiacal sign ruled my the sun) *Ditmars* (7 letters, containing the planet mars) ... 777. (moon and sun and mars) ... Also, numerologically, his name added up to 99 (the highest power number). And, what's really strange, is that I had no idea about this when we named him!

Evidently, I was forever effected by my preoccupation with the occult philosophies of popular Cabala. I recall the vows unto the order, and how they say that any initiate who breaks the silence regarding secrecy will be struck down and plagued with 'serious injury', 'insanity', or 'death'. Could it be, that when I finally told my psychiatrists about the order, I was actually negating the profundity of silence? Because, when it came right down to it, silence from the voices was all I craved.

I MUST HAVE BEEN BORN ON THE WRONG SIDE OF HISTORY
CHAPTER 31

ENSUING THE BIRTH OF MY SON, GABRIEL LEONARD DITMARS, I PRO-
ceeded to struggle. In the first two and a half years of his life, I was hospi-
talized half a dozen times. My recollection of these events and the crisis
situations that surrounded them, to be fair, were a little bit blurry, compounded by repeated changes in medication, and dosage, and tobacco,
and marijuana, and dietary adjustments. I was just riding the waves, cast
adrift in the vast ocean of Samsara. If hell did exist on the earth, I found it!

Considering that several fully trained medical doctors and clinicians
had told me, point-blank, that I had a severe mental illness and that I
would need to take meds for the rest of my life, it is perhaps surprising
to note that my denial clouded my eyes and I stubbornly resisted this
verdict. But, it just sounded like such a death sentence.

Having received the diagnosis from Doctor S (upon my first hospitalization), and having fired Doctor W (anon my second hospitalization)
because he disapproved of vitamin therapy, I was taken in by Doctor T
W. I began seeing her at her Vancouver office. Then, my wife and son and
I spent the summer at the ranch in the Nicola Valley. I was in charge of

some carpentry projects and shovelling the manure that the horses left behind. Every single day, every single hour, I heard the voice of the Dalai Lama, as though he was watching me. *He's Maitreya! The future buddha! I have no doubt.* I was taking sixteen pills a day.

On our return to the coast, after those few summer months of 2003, we spent one month on Saltspring Island. I was off my meds, after trying homeopathic remedies, and after taking Ayurvedic medicine, and after a considerable amount of time avoiding bread and dairy. Slowly, over the course of October, my delusions returned, concluding my temporary honeymoon period.

And, though I can't quite remember the actual course of events, I do know that I ended up in the psych ward, as a direct result of going off my meds suddenly. I recall how my own friends and my own family members, in spite of their unconditional love, were hesitant to see me during my stays at both UBC Hospital and Vancouver General Hospital. I remember that I had lost a lot of weight, and failed to maintain a healthy hygiene. I was also hearing voices. I remember how scary it was to believe that the nurses and patients were vampires. The voices were providing codenames such as *Master, Slave,* or *Immortal.*

Now, after I was discharged around January of 2004, I moved into a sublet apartment in Strathcona. Once again, I was smoking cigarettes, and making tape recordings of my life. I also had delusions about the person who was subletting the bachelor pad to me. I ended up getting evicted from there, and moving into a warehouse dungeon called 'The Monster'.

Down there, near Commercial and Hastings, I shaved my head, and started smoking Drum tobacco and huge amounts of marijuana. Every day. All day. It was a deadly lifestyle, if I do say so myself. But, the THC and nicotine and adrenaline that was pumping through my veins kept me hungry for whatever trash life was throwing at me. I was high.

Never in my wildest dreams did I imagine a more unhealthy and spiritually detrimental existence. For four hundred dollars a month, I was given a box to live in, surrounded by secondhand smoke. It was a warehouse full of pot-smoking punks in an industrial district on the east-side. But, there were perks, which was why I continued living there for several months.

And, I continued seeing Doctor T W. She had me on 800 milligrams of Seroquel. I recorded, night and day, 'albums' of spontaneous epic free-style verse. Disc after disc, I accumulated cd's full of the stuff. My psychiatrist knew about my marijuana use, but continued seeing me once every two weeks or so. She warned me to stay away from my wife, because her verbal abuse caused me to regress into psychosis.

Regardless, and in spite of the unhealthy environment, my wife and son visited me there once or twice. The anti-psychotics I was taking were very powerful. And, I struggled to maintain anything remotely resembling healthy sleep habits. After all, I was up all night, recording directly onto my portable cd recorder.

Completely out of the blue, the woman who lived upstairs got into an argument with me, and ordered me to leave. She wanted me gone by the end of the month, but I insisted that I would be gone that day. So, I packed up all my belongings (paintings, books, tapes, cd's, clothes, furniture, and cell phone), and asked my brother to give me the use of his truck to move across town and back into our mother's apartment.

I remember the night of June 30th, 2004, when I had a disagreement with her, and wandered off into the night. First, with new sandals on my feet, I walked to the liquor store, bought a bottle of red wine, and walked to my favourite restaurant, treated myself to a vegetarian dinner, and walked all the way to Wreck Beach. By the time I got there, it was well after midnight and my wine bottle was almost empty.

So, early on the morning of Canada Day, I thought I was living in a holographic universe. In the moonlight, I bathed my sore feet in the ocean, hearing the voices. *He's a super-computer! I wonder if he knows how important he really is. Bowie and the Lama are convinced that he is the one. He's insanely gorgeous! That's all there is to it.*

Searching for meaning in my meaningless world, I stayed awake all that night, hallucinating voices and visions. Then, around sunrise, as the sky began to brighten, I dried off my feet, put my sandals back on, and began walking east. Past UBC, past the golf course, along 10th avenue. Around Sasamat, I was completely convinced that I had huge archangelic wings on my shoulders.

Up and down hills, all over town, I was refusing to answer the calls I was receiving on my cell phone. Then, when I got to Strathcona, the warm sun was high in the sky, and I sat down in the grass to call my brother. He convinced me to meet him at a restaurant on Commercial Drive. I thought my mom and dad were working for the FBI and CIA. But, I felt that I was able to trust my brother.

So, I met with him. The ambulance was there. I was driven to VGH, and admitted. Again.

THE ONE HUNDREDTH MAN

CHAPTER 32

HAD I ENOUGH COMMON SENSE, I PROBABLY WOULDN'T HAVE WALKED all night and all morning in sandals that were not yet broken in. They were brand new Birkenstocks, and they preformed murder on my poor feet. I remember walking into the intensive care unit, with my toes and heels all scraped and bloody from walking all across the city.

I was convinced that Michael Jackson was watching me closely over some sort of video surveillance. *He's the next big supermodel! Look at him! He really doesn't even know that he's world famous!* With voices of celebrities running through my mind, I did as I was asked and got changed into the uniform hospital pyjamas. The nurses showed me to my bedroom, where another young man also had his bed. I thought he was the reincarnation of Rimbaud. He liked to talk. So, I went into the lounge area, and fielded a few phone calls. One from my dad, one from my mom, and one from my brother.

Landing finally on one of the couches, perched over a coffee table on which there was a jigsaw puzzle unfinished, I stared vacantly at the pieces, ogling at how they all fit together. The hospital food was garbage, I must say. Microwaved shepherds pie did little good for me, but the meds were working wonders. Within a matter of days, I was feeling centred and thinking clearly. Who cared if I was the next big supermodel? Who cared if my roommate was formerly the author of 'A Season In Hell'? I had to look at the grim reality of it all. I was in the psych ward again, and my one priority was to be let free to go home.

Reapplying fresh new bandages on my blistered feet, I tried my very best to look sane. I moved calmly. I dressed appropriately. I ate a decent amount. I was polite with all the nurses. But, my crazy eyes gave it all away. Still psychotic, I wasn't hallucinating archangel wings on my back, but my wily gaze told the whole entire story.

Outside of the ICU, on the patio for my five minutes of fresh air, I swore beneath my breath, cursing the fact that I was labeled insane. Eventually, responding to meds, I went to the main psychiatric ward of VGH, located in a separate, older building. This time, my roommate was a big man with a low IQ, a friendly giant. His bed and my bed were divided by a curtain. I still felt like the world was ending, and that I was responsible. Yet, every single time a stranger asked me for my name, I was somehow disappointed to see that either they truly didn't know who I was or that they were pretending not to acknowledge my universal infamy.

Yes, my wife and toddler son came to the ward one day to visit me. It filled me with emotion. Love. Anger. Pity. But, above all else, I felt embarrassed. They only stayed for a short while, but were relieved to see that I was safe. The voices of famous people continued. Soon, I was convinced that I had brain cancer. Once again, the doctors and nurses were misleading me. It was all a ploy. A conspiracy. A false reality.

JUST PART OF THE ONE PERCENT
CHAPTER 33

ON THE ONE HAND, THE '1%' REFERS TO THE RATIO OF EXTREME wealth. On the other hand, the '1%' refers to the occurrence of severe schizophrenia. The irony is that, diagnosed with the paranoid delusional disorder, one of my most persistent delusions is that I'm a billionaire. For the past fourteen years, I've hallucinated voices telling me that I'm a 'billionaire'. And, on the third hand, both statistics refer directly to an *anomaly* existing in the human population. But, the voices always see it as a 'good' thing to be filthy rich. As though it were something to strive for and be desired.

My argument consistently states that I don't want to be world famous. I don't want to be a billionaire. I don't want to produce 'gold record' after 'gold record'. I don't want to be a supermodel. I don't want to be bigger than Bill Gates. But, the voices I hear every day are proceeding to make these false assumptions.

Except, my thirteen year old son would love it if his dad drove a shiny red sports car, instead of taking the bus. His mom would also love it if I transformed my art into millions and bought a big house for them to live in. But, the statistics are all against me on this one. Only '1%' of artists achieve fame.

Now, I have no idea just what to think about all this. All I know is that, even now, after David Bowie's death, I'm still hearing his voice daily. Rumour has it that Bowie (who just happens to have made billions) is going to be releasing albums posthumously. My psychiatrist believes that I myself will achieve posthumous fame. As I said before, he told me that I'm like Van Gogh, only I still have both my ears.

BEETHOVEN LIVED AND DIED LONG BEFORE HEARING-AIDS WERE INVENTED
CHAPTER 34

LITTLE GOOD IT DID ME TO CONTEMPLATE THE FACT THAT IF JESUS were alive today he'd be considered a madman. And, like most other madmen in this military industrial complex called Canada, he would probably spend some time in a psychiatric hospital. I mean, really. I can just imagine it: the reincarnation of Christ, standing on the street corner at Main and Hastings, claiming that he is hearing the voice of God. Locked up. Diagnosed. Given meds. Monitored. And, Jesus Christ himself would also be given pyjamas to wear.

Eventually, I was discharged from VGH. But, not before I was given a new psychiatrist. Doctor E took me into his office, and urged me to start seeing him. Apparently, he practiced both in Vancouver (where my mother and brother lived) and the Sunshine Coast (where my wife and son were living), and he promised me the best of treatment.

So, Doctor E discharged me out of the hospital and into his care. The only problem was that I was on only 200 milligrams of Seroquel (one quarter of what I should have been taking). I was appearing very 'normal' in those days, though still waters ran deep.

Sleeping well, eating well, grooming myself well, and able to articulate well, my internalized symptoms were falling under the radar. Secretly, I believed I was the messiah. Everything I perceived pointed to that conclusion, though everyone who cared for me told me otherwise. Doctor E gave me a business card, and scheduled my first appointment.

Reality set in. My wife arranged it so that the three of us would move to a basement suite on the Sunshine Coast. We received our first cheque for a family on disability, and packed up all our belongings into the back of my brother's white van, and drove off into the rainy, dark, and cold November night.

Except, I really shouldn't have been driving. On the ferry ride, I was crying and sobbing, in tears while in the driver's seat. Then, from Langdale, we drove to Roberts Creek, and picked up the house key from a trusty neighbour. With our clothing soaked from the deluge, we entered the sliding glass ground floor door, and switched on the light. It was a beautiful two bedroom flat. But, I was unable to enjoy it, because the voices were in my ears. Sometimes, I envy Beethoven's deafness.

Now, preoccupied by what life was demanding of me, I neglected to return the big white van to my brother. Naturally, he became very worried. After about one week, he and our mother came looking for me. But, when I heard them knocking on the door, I was busy with recording more spontaneous epic verse into the microphone. Quickly, I took off my headphones, and ran towards them, where they stood in the kitchen. I was growling loudly and violently. I felt like I was slipping into my Mozart personality again. Throwing another fit.

Doing all he could to diffuse the situation, my brother stopped me in my tracks, held my arms and legs tightly, and brought me to the floor of the bedroom. He has always been bigger and stronger than me. And, though I struggled briefly, my strength was no match for him. Breathing heavily, sweating, and sobbing, we sat down on the carpet, fatigued by stress.

Eventually, I was admitted to Saint Mary's Hospital, and confined to isolation in the psych ward. All I wanted to do was write and record. But, I was there in a room resembling a prison cell, twiddling my thumbs obsessively. My wife brought me a plate of fresh vegetables, which I ate ravenously. Then, after about 36 hours, a nurse came into the room, with pills in one hand and a cup of water in the other. I refused to take the meds. She insisted that I should. And, after much deliberation, we compromised on half the dosage. She told me that I was needing to return to VGH.

Return I did. After a long ambulance ride, strapped into a stretcher, from Sechelt, to Langdale, then on the ferry to Horseshoe Bay, and then finally to Vancouver, I returned to VGH. I returned to the vampires. I returned to the aliens. I returned to the hellish hospital food. I returned, without my wife and son. Last but not least, I returned to Doctor E, who did not see any reason for my stay. So, if memory serves me correctly, I was discharged in under a week, and sent back to Roberts Creek.

Each day, my wife and I were arguing. I was really not myself. Around Christmas, I was mute. Two psych nurses came to do a home visit. They interviewed me, asking question after question. I replied by writing notes on paper. They left, seeing no reason to continue the interview. Once again, I was falling between the cracks in the mental health system. I eventually emerged from my mutism, and we had a fairly good Christmas. Gabriel and I would play a game we called 'sword-fight', and bonded in the way fathers and sons do.

Did I love my wife and son? Yes. Was I able to express it? Not really. I was too preoccupied with listening to the voices. *Gautama is the code-word! He's made it to 10=1, the grade of Ippisimus! The messiah is in that man! He is anointed, and she is a vampire! And, it's true love, no less!*

A SOJOURN BACK INTO THE BUSH
CHAPTER 35

DID I EXPERIENCE HALLUCINATIONS? YES. DID I KNOW THAT THEY were hallucinations? Absolutely not! I believed they were real. Had I fallen away from the Golden Dawn? Yes, fully. Had I forgotten about my brothers and sisters in the great work? Not at all. I remember one particular session of recording my spontaneous epic verse, during which I had my eyes closed in front of the microphone, when suddenly I imagined the greatly honoured chief standing behind me, pointing a loaded gun directly at my head.

What did I do? I continued singing. But, it was scary. Because, I thought it was real. And, right around that time, in January of 2005, my wife and I got into another argument. She locked me out of the house, at about 3:00 in the morning. I told her to let me in the door. But, all she did was open the window and yell at me. I joined her near the window-sill, and asked her if she was a supermodel. She denied it. But, instead of calling the ambulance, she ended up letting me into the house, and we fought. I grabbed her wrists, and hung on tight. Then, she called 911, and reported domestic violence.

An RCMP officer came, and told me that I could go to jail or to hospital. I chose the hospital. But, since I checked myself in voluntarily, I could check myself out voluntarily. I spent the night in Saint Mary's, and returned to the streets of Sechelt first thing the very next morning.

Returning to Vancouver, I began living with my mother once more. I spent all my time in her basement, recording. And, I started painting in the patio outside. Then, the unspeakable occurred. I discovered a box of baseball cards that used to belong to my mother's father. I knew they were worth a pretty penny, and slowly, methodically, organized them and sold them. For a little more than two grand. Then, somehow, I managed to lease a brand new black Honda Civic. And, I believed that by selling the baseball cards and leasing a car, I was causing the global stock market to crash.

From there, I left town, and drove to Rainbow Lake. My dad and his wife had since moved to a small town in the interior. And, the ranch was left vacant. As I grew nearer to the property, cruising down the old dirt logging roads, I came to one of the driveways, which was blocked off by a huge stone boulder. I got out of the car, and tried to move it. *Look at the messiah! He has super powers! But, even the great miracle worker can't budge it with his bare hands!* I got back into the vehicle, and drove, eventually finding the right road. I drove towards the back gate, and brought all my stuff into the house. My cd recorder, my microphone. My speakers. My art portfolio. My various belongings. I had everything I needed, except my mind.

My memory of this time spent in the bush is pretty vague. All I know for sure is that I was hallucinating 24/7. Voices, and visions. Galore! I wrote constantly, and made dozens of hourlong recordings. I even produced a 729 day calendar. My most vivid memory is of standing there in the loft of the house, with my eyes closed in front of the microphone, singing, and believing that I had been voted in to what the voices of David Bowie called 'The Royal Academy'. I saw myself seated in the back of the balcony overlooking what seemed like the academy awards ceremony. Everyone was clapping for me.

I heard the voices chorus now: *He's the one! A real male prodigy! Genelle is a god! The members of the royal academy are giving him a standing ovation! His intelligent quotient is exponential! He's not insane! He's brilliant!*

So, on and on it went, until one day a police officer arrived at the door, with two men from town. They brought me outside to the police car, and got me on the radio phone with my dad's wife. She was making sure that I was okay. Was I okay? No. Did I seem okay? Well, I must have, because the police car drove away as soon as it had arrived, and without altercation. I went back to my recordings.

Continuing to clean the house from top to bottom, pretty soon I got the inspiration to do some early spring gardening. After digging up the soil, I drove all the way to Bella Coola, in order to buy some seeds to plant. Carrots, beets, chard, kale, lettuce, and various other vegetables. I thought the world was ending, but God was up in heaven gardening.

How long I was up there, I'm still not sure. But, after filling up every page with ink and disc with music, and with both gardens planted, I decided to leave. From the ranch, I drove to Anahim Lake, and made a trip to the gas station. I filled up the tank of the car with regular unleaded, and bought a lottery ticket. I thought that winning the lottery was the only way I could get paid the millions I thought I deserved. I thought I was on a military mission.

I drove to Williams Lake, and filled up on gas again. I was in a bit of a hurry, because I needed to be back in Sechelt by the 31st of May, to attend a court proceeding that had resulted from the domestic violence incident involving my wife. Escaping from the bush, I was forgetting to eat. I was also very dehydrated. Not to mention delusional. But, no one showed any concern. The previous October, I had hitch-hiked all the way to the ranch and back, perceived by strangers as crazy. While I was there in the fall, my wife and son actually came all the way to visit me. Now, with a car in my possession, I was seen as normal. But, normal I was not.

Each hour that passed, on that long drive south, I contemplated what the voices were saying. But, the more I paid attention to them, the louder they grew. Until, I finally arrived in Vancouver. Instead of going to my mother's apartment, I parked the car near the beach, and slept in the driver's seat.

From there, early the next morning, I had a Mars bar for breakfast, and proceeded in the general direction of the Sunshine Coast. On my way to the courthouse, I listened as the voices raged on and on: *He's a criminal!*

He's criminally insane! Look at how fast he's driving! A real male prodigy, but also a real maniac! Look at him go!

THE END OF THE WORLD AS I KNEW IT
CHAPTER 36

MY WHOLE WORLD CAME CRUMBLING DOWN AROUND ME, ON THE morning of May 31st, 2005. I imagined that I was completely responsible for all world events, both in and around my own life. With only a chocolate bar for sustenance, I continued past the breakfast hour, anxious as all hell, and arrived on the Sunshine Coast, ready for battle. If I were a religious man, I would say that this 'battle' was between me and the devil. But, for me, it took a slightly different shape.

I was battling against my own personal creations, in the world of both my art and writing, and among my friends and the members of my family. My mother was perhaps the most concerned. She had scheduled an appointment with Doctor W, seeing as Doctor E had quit on me. I hadn't seen any psychiatrist in almost three whole months. And, my poor mom was just crossing her fingers that I would make it to see Doctor W before anything terrible happened. The appointment was for the afternoon of June 1st.

So, let it be known that, for reasons outlined in this chapter, I never made it to that appointment. To tell the truth, I was kind of dreading the thought of getting the intramuscular injection that Doctor W was going to prescribe. But, mostly, the thought of maintaining my mental health just wasn't the first thing on my mind.

Conceiving vast elaborate conspiracies and suspicions of an alien invasion, I thought I was on a mission sponsored by the FBI, the CIA, and the RCMP. I felt focused. But, I was focused on the wrong thing. My main focus was around trying to appease the famous and powerful people behind the voices. Memories of recently living with my wife, lying in the sunlight on the ground in the south-facing yard by the sea, with my two year old son on my naked chest, believing that I owned half the planet, while Osama Bin Laden owned the other half, these memories and more came flooding back into my brain, as I drove.

Each moment that passed was a moment closer to imminent and inevitable fatality. I thought my own life was at risk. And, honestly, it kinda was. Me and my black sedan, together, we were going the wrong way on a oneway track.

Like a bat out of hell, I drove speeding down the rural highway and roads, through Langdale, through Gibsons, through Roberts Creek, past Half-moon Bay, and all the way to Sechelt. I parked my car outside the courthouse, and walked on up to the door. I was dressed like an ordinary eccentric, but my version of 'eccentric' wasn't at all 'ordinary'.

Look! The insane criminal is entering the courthouse! He's dressed like someone from Bowie's entourage! It's about time we find out if he's a man or a mongrel! Maybe, he's neither one. He's a myth! He's a madman! He's the messiah!

And, so the voices went. After waiting impatiently for more than half an hour, I finally found my lawyer. I forget his name. But, whatever it was, I had a delusion surrounding him. Somehow, the voices were telling me that he was the reincarnation of one of my father's former enemies from a past life. I didn't like him.

Now, the picture became plain. He informed me that my wife was neglecting to appear in court. He told me that she didn't want to have anything to do with me. Ever again! I struggled to maintain the focus on my military mission. I didn't say a word, and was out the door.

Emerging from the courthouse through the same door I had entered, I turned around, beneath the flag of British Columbia and the flag of

Canada, and gave the middle finger to the surveillance cameras. I was angry that the provincial court system was upholding the rights of my wife above my own. I was the messiah. She was an extraterrestrial vampire from another dimension. I also had a belief that she had an evil twin with whom she traded places with on a daily basis. I thought that the evil twin was poisoning my son with her breastmilk.

On the outside, I was back in the driver seat, with one thing on my mind: the total systematic annihilation of all the vampires and aliens from the Sunshine Coast. Beginning with my wife. I still don't know just how all this made sense to me at the time. But, none-the-less, I believed it, with every single ounce of my total brain mass. A madman with strong convictions is a dangerous thing.

Under my breath, I began talking back to the voices. All this, while speeding down the highway, in the direction of Roberts Creek. I remembered how to get to the house. After all, I *did* live there before. Nine Inch Nails was playing loudly on the car stereo. I heard Trent Reznor's voice telling me that he was my brother. I also heard the voice of a certain local singer-songwriter, who told me that she was my sister. They both insisted that I carry out the mission, and they promised me millions of dollars.

So, on I went, parked the car outside of the house, and barged in. I found a note on the table in the front room. It was addressed to someone named Brandon. Immediately, I falsely assumed that this 'Brandon' was my twin sibling. My double. There was a red heart drawn in pencil crayon, and it was signed by my wife (or who I *thought* was my wife).

From that moment onwards, it was one big blur. I barged in through the sliding glass door, through the living room, past Gabriel's bedroom that was full of brightly coloured toys, and through the kitchen. After looking everywhere, I finally found them both in her bedroom. They were in the process of breastfeeding.

Really aggressive, violent, almost aggravated, I started punching her head with my fist. I made sure that Gabriel was a safe distance away, before I then proceeded to kick her and punch her and pull her hair and scream at her. Come to think of it, I wasn't sure just who 'she' was. Was she my wife? My ex-wife? An alien Grey? A vampire? A liar? An imposter? A whore? I honestly didn't have a clue.

And, during the assault, I remember looking over at the child. The blue eyed blonde haired boy, less than three years old, was crying as loud as he could, saying: *No, dada! Nooo!* Back then, he only knew four words to begin with. 'Yes', 'No', 'Mom', and 'Dad'. He was using fifty percent of his limited vocabulary, all with the strong intention to tell me what not to do. At that moment, I felt myself looking away from her and towards him. He distracted me just enough to allow her to get away.

Gone from the room, she went upstairs to tell the neighbours to call the police. Then, I picked up Gabriel, who by this time was in tears, quite traumatized in fact. He was completely naked. The strange thing was that he knew me as his father. And, fathers should be strong and solid. But, I felt like such a failure. All I knew was that he and I needed to get away. Away from her, away from all the vampires on the Sunshine Coast, away from all the world of cameras and video surveillance. The insanity of global politics... But I digress.

My initial impulse was to save and protect my son. So, I brought him outside and put him in the car. Then, I ran back into the house to retrieve some of my art. By that time, the neighbour had retrieved Gabriel and brought him into the house. Then, getting up from out of the small room that had been my office studio, I ran out into the kitchen. It was at that very moment that I realized an RCMP officer was pointing a taser at me. He threatened me with 50, 000 volts of electricity if I didn't comply.

Exclaiming loudly, he ordered me down on the ground with my hands behind my back. The only reason I complied was because I thought that the policeman was taking me to jail to award me millions of dollars once we got back to the station.

Now, most criminals complain about police brutality. But, looking back on that day, more than ten years ago, I am extremely *thankful* that I was arrested! As far as I'm concerned, my arrest was the best thing that could have happened. The officer who did the honours probably saved my life, my son's life, and my wife's life. None-the-less, I was handcuffed and ankle-cuffed, and locked into the backseat of the car.

The whole drive back to Sechelt, where I had been earlier that day, I was completely psychotic. Somehow, I felt as though I was driving the vehicle. I received telepathic messages from the officer, whose face I could see reflected in the rearview mirror.

Suddenly, before I knew what was happening, I was brought into the jail, stripped of all my clothes, photographed, and dragged into one of the cells. I remember lying there, completely motionless, on my back, stark nude, with a head full of hair. They had taken my silver earrings out. I rested there for approximately one hour.

Or, was it an eternity? I don't know. All I knew was that my mind was racing. Thousands of profound thoughts per second. Visions of George W. Bush and my mother in law fighting over custody of my son. Psychedelic images of distant constellations. And, suddenly, the voices were saying that the IQ of the prison guard was 81. The fact that 81 is the square of 9 seemed all-important.

From then on, I demonstrated several elements of acute psychosis. Some catatonia. Some paranoia. Signs of a suffering soul. I thought that the jail cell was some sort of elevator, and I was descending down towards the centre of the earth, as part of some sort of cosmic experiment. The numbers '10' and '4' seemed especially significant. I was becoming more and more lost, without even budging an inch.

Now, the food came. I didn't touch it. And, in retrospect, I wonder as to why they didn't give me any antipsychotic medication. If I had been a diabetic, I would have needed my insulin. I was a schizophrenic and I needed my Seroquel.

On the same note, I really think this topic should be raised as a major issue with regards to rights of prisoners. A diabetic would suffer without insulin. I was suffering because my meds weren't given to me. The really bizarre thing to contemplate is that I had been taking my meds. Exactly as prescribed, in fact. It just wasn't enough. My previous psychiatrist, Dr. E, was happy with how I was doing at 100 milligrams at bedtime, when in truth I should have probably been taking 800.

Not knowing who I was, not knowing where I was, not knowing was painful. But, it was not nearly as bad as I had feared. Years later, I learned that my wife and son were safe. She had suffered from mostly scrapes and bruises. Thank god that it wasn't worse. I mean, my psychosis had gotten completely out of hand. I could easily have killed someone. I hurt the two people whom I had loved more than any other people on the planet. If that's not a sure sign of 'illness', I don't know what is!

So, there I was, in the cell, talking to myself, thinking that I was a man named 'SA', a former pilot for the royal navy. I took a seat on the toilet, speaking to the world I thought was listening. Then, I had thoughts of causing a scene by banging my head against the concrete walls.

Except, no one was watching. I felt like I was world famous, and yet completely ignored and neglected. How could a man be so well known and yet also be so unrecognized? Even to this day, a decade later, I find myself musing absently over this very question.

No human contact did I get during the time which I estimate to have been two days. If there was a hell, I had found it. And, it got even more hellish when they transferred me from the Sechelt jail to North Fraser Pretrial. The transportation alone must have been costing taxpayers thousands of dollars. And, from one maximum security locker to another, I was forced to sit quietly behind bars for what seemed like days, being thrown all sorts of cold paper bag lunches and nothing to drink.

Soon, I arrived at the corrections institute out in one of the suburbs. They showed me to my bed, where I slept, and hallucinated for seven days, not moving, not eating, and sipping only occasionally from the fountain. I was pretty much catatonic. I was retreating inwards, rebelling from the sinister plot of the world outside.

I listened to the moans and groans of the other inmates. Sounds of hell, I was sure. Then, on the morning of the eighth day, I was escorted by one of the guards to a psychiatrist's office on site. He interviewed me in some depth, asking me what I was thinking. I told him that I was dreaming of a place called 'Bedlam', where all the whores were kept. He asked me what I wanted. I told him that I wanted to make use of my telepathic abilities, by signing on to a contract with the Federal Bureau of Investigation.

Can you believe it? And, I said it with a straight face, totally sober. Then, after the interview was over, the doctor told me that he was sending me to F.P.I. *Hallelujah!* I thought to myself. You see, I though he said 'FBI', and I thought that I was being taken by paddy wagon to a job interview. How very wrong I was! It was actually Forensic Psychiatric Institute.

And, arriving at the final destination, the officers led me into a maximum security facility of some sort. They took my cuffs off, and led me down a long hallway into a cafeteria. They fed me a huge plate of food. I consumed it, down to the very last breadcrumb.

Later on, they showed me to my bed. I thought I was on a spaceship, and that I was captain of the intergalactic mission to travel through time. I got dressed into a red shirt and blue sweatpants, and fell sound asleep.

When I slept in the next morning, oblivious to the breakfast bell, the nurses weren't too surprised. I emerged from the bedroom just before noon, and made my way to the television room. I sat down, and watched whatever was on. And, I continued doing just that for an entire month.

I believed that the other people on my ward were holograms. So, I didn't interact with any of them, because I thought it was some sort of test. Every morning, I was the first one in line for breakfast, and the first one to finish my plate. Then, I watched tv all morning. Then, lunchtime. Then, more tv. Then, dinnertime. Then, more tv. Then, (and this was the best part of it all), they gave me meds to take. 100 milligrams of Seroquel, precisely what I had been on at the time of the violent incident.

So, I also refused to bathe. My fingernails were growing long, and my beard was becoming bushier. I was focused on surviving the end of the world. I did this by trying to 'ground' the sonar. I thought that Tom Cruise was going to walk into my room any minute, and offer me millions of dollars and a handshake. Apparently, in my delusional world, my former wife and the famous actor were going to congratulate me on the discovery of time travel.

Death. The scent of it. Hell. The putrid warmth of it. I was made to take part in physical activities when the 19 other men on the ward participated in volleyball and floor hockey. I went with them every time, but all I did was sit cross-legged in the corner of the gymnasium, sulking at all the insults that the voices were throwing.

Old Bryn-Bo! He hasn't said a single word since his admission. Except to the nurses, the doctors, and the therapists. He just needs to ground the sonar. In order to end the war. Can he do it? He's the one! He has to do it! For all our sakes! He's the only cadet who has attained the ability to ground high levels of magnetic sonar!

My condition was still very critical. But, I slowly gained back the weight that I had lost. People came to visit me. My mother had been so very worried about me. She must have lost a lot of sleep over my suffering. She was probably thinking: 'If only he had made it to June 1st!'

WALKING AROUND THE BLOCK

CHAPTER 37

CURRENTLY, IT IS THE END OF JANUARY, AND MY SMOKING HABIT HAS returned. No more vaporizer, no more nicotine liquid, no more batteries, no more tanks, no more coils, no more failed attempts at burning propylene glycol. In some ways, I feel better. In some ways, I feel worse. For seven days now, I've been smoking an additive-free brand of whole leaf Canadian cigarettes called North Fields.

On my walk around the block this morning, I had another one. A man in a wheelchair asked me to light his smoke, and I did. Then, after telling him to have a good day, I continued on my dizzy way, stumbling down along 6th avenue. Finally, back to my building.

My apartment is nice and warm. It felt good to come in from the cold outside. Now, I am seated at my desk, writing, as I recall the details of my last hospitalization.

Memory serves me well, as I remember the suffering which I endured in the summer months at the Forensic Psychiatric Hospital. I remember wearing a red shirt each and every day for the month of June, spending copious amounts of time watching television. I remember wearing a blue shirt each and every day for the month of July, spending the majority of my time horizontal in bed.

On one occasion, while watching television in a red shirt, a young man walked into the room. He had a shaved head, and a tattoo of a teardrop on his upper cheek. He must have been about twenty years old. As he searched for a video to watch, I looked at him suspiciously. I believed him to be my son, Gabriel, time travelling from the future. In my delusion, I thought he was trying to track down his father.

Now, this particular delusion is really quite fascinating. Because, regardless of the fact that it seemed to prove that time travel was possible, it was all under the assumption that, sometime in the future, I would be dead, before Gabriel really got to know me. I knew that my son was still a toddler, with very few permanent memories of his father. But, time travel was taken for granted in among the themes of my delusional reality. I thought the man who entered the television room was my son in search of his long lost (lost to suicide) father.

Grim days were spent that summer, watching television, thinking the patients were holographic projections devised to test me. And, then, after weeks of not bathing, with my hair and nails quite long and overgrown, I retired to my room, where I slept for nearly twenty-one hours every day.

Each day, I just lay there, dressed in a blue shirt, drifting in and out of sleep, thinking I was saving the world by grounding sonar. The voices continued, night and day: *Look at him laying there! He has brain cancer. We're sure.* When the voices had diagnosed me with 'brain cancer', it was really quite frightening. But, part of the delusion was that I was the only person in the world to have the cure for the disease.

Now, the key thing to be aware of is that the delusional thinking makes no sense now, but that my thoughts seemed to make perfect sense at the time. I still believed that I was the messiah. It's just that this 'messiah' was suffering from cancer. And, also HIV.

Early on in my 'blue shirt phase', I remember lying in bed, my eyes half-open, believing that my friends and family members were all in prison because of me. I was sure that Brittany Spears was in the room upstairs, taking care of Gabriel, seeing as his mom was in no state to care for a child. All day, like background noise, I heard my wife screaming deliriously. And, yet, the other version of my wife was time travelling with Tom Cruise. Both realities seemed just as viable to me.

Then, the miraculous happened.

I had my eyes open slightly. I looked over towards the door, and saw my toddler son walk in. Blue eyes and blonde hair and all, he motioned bravely towards the bed. Then, he pointed at me, and said something that broke my heart: *That not bad dada. That good dada.* And, he smiled. I thought he was there as a test to see if the man in the bed was in fact a criminal or simply mentally ill.

Cherubic young Gabriel, he seemed so very real at the time. But, I now know it was a hallucination, both visual and auditory. I pointed at him, and he touched my hand. Then, I fell back to sleep again.

Could I discern the difference between dream and reality? No, not in those days. I didn't even know who I was. Late one night near the end of July, I was crying alone in my room, huddled in the corner, feeling very afraid. Not knowing what else to do, I ran down the long sterile neon hallway towards the nursing station. I exclaimed, in tears: *I don't know who I am!*

His Holiness the Dalai Lama would have considered this simply a symptom of being human. But, I knew better. It was insanity.

And, pretty soon, one of the nurses on duty came fearfully out from behind the safety glass door. In his trembling hand, there was a small pill of Ativan. With tears streaming down both my cheeks, I tried to explain to him that Ativan was 'hard on the heart'. And, because of this, I refused to take it, even though it probably would have helped.

Returning to my solitary cell, I calmed myself down, and curled up in the blankets, longing for sleep. Eventually, I got to sleep, and escaped into realms of dream. As a matter of plain fact, the dreams I dreamed at night were less surreal than my waking life. And, my waking life was a nightmare!

Again, I woke, and again I slept the day away. More symptoms of paranoia and delusion ensued. *He's bigger than Bill Gates! Does he know how important he is? Everyday, there's gold record after gold record!* I ate breakfast, and the voices would say: *Another gold record!* I had a nap, and the voices would say: *Another gold record!* I ate lunch, and the voices would say: *Another gold record!* Over and over again and again, the voices said: *Another gold record! Another gold record! Another gold record!* But, you get the idea.

Counting my blessings, billionaire or not, the one thing I knew was that I was safe. And, that knowledge was probably the only thing that enabled my friends and family members to sleep peacefully at night. My mother came to visit once a week or so. And, once she brought my old friend, The Buddha, with her. He gave me a prayer bracelet. Then, my father and my brother came, and we played (you guessed it)... ping-pong! Ah yes, the ultimate measure of true sanity. And, once, my dad's wife, Jen, came to visit me, and gave me six bottles of drinking water. But, I was convinced that giving or receiving anything was a telltale sign that I had HIV.

The messiah has the High Virus! The anointed one has brain cancer! But, remains immune! Let's hope he has the cure to these diseases! The hope of the entire world is in his hands! If and when he cuts his fingernails, he should sell the trimmings to Madonna for a pretty penny! She'd be the one to have them! We're certain, he's the saviour!

Eventually, nearing the end of my two month assessment period, a social worker came to visit me. She was rambling on and on about this and that (namely my future). But, my cognitive abilities were very poor. So, I told her that I wasn't comprehending anything that she was saying, and she left.

Realistically, my fate was resting completely in the hands of the provincial government. But, my delusions presented arguments that the exact opposite was true. Was I a special agent, on an international military mission? No. I was a mentally ill young man who had hit the lowest point in his life.

I was having lunch in the cafeteria one day, hearing voices. I was laughing out loud, between bites. And, I was very close to standing up from my chair and declaring that I was a male witch! As far as I recall, I didn't say a word, and simply returned to laughing and eating what was left on my plate. I should also mention that after each and every meal, the nurses would count the knives and forks, to prevent people from using them as weapons.

Someone on my ward, a man in his fifties, had been arrested for beating his own dear mother with a walking cane, and claimed that he had documentation proving that he owned a whopping one percent of the world's oil. By promising other patients some of the share of the stock on the outside, he succeeded in getting favours from people left right and centre.

The time I spent during the two months of assessment was accompanied by many experiences reminiscent of "One Flew Over The Cookoo's Nest". The patients there, on Ash One ward, some were criminals, and some were simply deranged. In early August, I was given an intramuscular injection of an anti-psychotic medication known as Piportil.

I wanted it to work. I wanted the voices to go away. I wanted to not live my life as though I was the messiah. I wanted it all to just go away. I wanted to wake up from my nightmare. Of course, I thought they were implanting microscopic nanobots into my body. But, I was optimistic that they were honestly trying to help me. For this, I was grateful, even though the needle hurt like hell.

Come injection time, they led me down a long hallway to a padded cell. There was a mattress lying on the floor, where they asked me to lie down on my belly and pull down my pants. I was horrified. I couldn't believe they were expecting me to do that. So, I demanded that they put the needle into my shoulder muscle instead.

Seeing just how desperate I was, they agreed. While I stood there, relaxing my arm, the nurse used the syringe, and injected the med. There was a little bit of blood, but nothing alarming. I even got a bandaid.

GOD AND GOD'S MUGSHOT
CHAPTER 38

SOMEWHERE IN THE FILES COLLECTED BY THE RCMP, THERE IS A PHO-tograph which the officers took of my face when they arrested me. I've never seen it. But, I'm pretty sure I'm not smiling in the picture.

Perhaps the medication they injected me with was a placebo. But, I doubt it. Never the less, I got the injection, and went to sleep. Almost as soon as I woke up, I noticed a distinct difference in my thought processes. Suddenly, I wasn't thinking about aliens or time travel or the FBI. I was just looking forward to breakfast. So, it's safe to say that I was responding robustly to the anti-psychotics.

And, the nurses noticed a change. When one of them served me scrambled eggs and toast, he asked me how I was doing. I actually made eye contact with him! This was a big improvement over my previous behaviour. I even asked him how *he* was doing. I felt like I had returned to my natural state of mind. The hallucinations gradually disappeared, and I was feeling much better.

Come lunchtime, we went outside into the small courtyard for some fresh air. Usually during these daily outdoor excursions, I would just lie down in the grass and remain motionless. But, this time, I went for a bit of a jog, running round the perimeter of the maximum security enclosure. The nurses took note of this, and they immediately took me in for questioning.

Eventually, they acknowledged my robust recovery, and transferred me from Ash One ward to Ash Two ward. I showered, and they gave me clean clothes to wear. And, in the new ward, I set up my bedroom, and realized that pretty much the only difference between the two wards was that smoking cigarettes was allowed on the new ward, whereas it wasn't allowed on the previous ward. But, I was not tempted.

All said, the other difference was that the Ash Two courtyard was considerably larger. But, they still counted the knives and forks when mealtime was over. I actually socialized with some of the other patients. Every Tuesday morning, they would give us each a twenty dollar bill, to spend on doughnuts and tobacco. I preferred to save the money.

God was on my side, after the injections took effect. I passed every test they threw at me. On one occasion, a dwarf woman came to measure my IQ. She said that my linguistic intelligence was exceptional. I could have told her that!

Eventually, with three square meals every day, I went from 144 pounds to 170 pounds of body weight. The medication also helped add some bulk to my fragile physical frame. When we went to the gym every other day, I even took part in the indoor volleyball. Meanwhile, I spent most of my time reflecting on my life.

Great strides were made for me in the months of August, September, and October. Nearly once a week, I would receive letters from the court system. Every time I needed to make a court appearance, they would transport me all the way from Port Coquitlam to Sechelt. And, fortunately, I was able to behave normally, instead of covering my ears and cowering.

One day, I received word from one of the nurses that I was going to be transferred to one of the houses on the property. It was called Hawthorne. Still a ward, but it came along with more freedom and more privileges. I had my own room, but had to share the rest of the house with three or four other men. Suddenly, I was allowed to use the gym anytime and go paint in the art studio anytime. It was weird to wear normal clothes again. I put my silver earrings back on, and asked my mother to bring some clothes for me to wear.

The lawyer showed me some photographs that were taken after the violent incident. My wife's face was covered with cuts and bruises. I just about cried, realizing what I had done. I just thanked my lucky stars that it hadn't been worse. My lawyer encouraged me to plead NCRMD, neither guilty nor innocent, but the legal version of 'insanity'. I agreed. And, I was found to be 'Not Criminally Responsible due to a Mental Disorder'. It was humiliating, to say the least, but necessary.

How I managed, I'm still not sure. But, I was exactly where I needed to be. I had food in my belly, a roof over my head, and clothes to wear. I was painting a lot, and playing basketball a lot. They even gave me a pedicure and took me to the dentist twice. However, the dentist appointments required me to sit in the chair with hand cuffs and ankle cuffs on. I was coping. And, every single day, I hoped and prayed that my wife and son were coping. I felt so very sorry. But, again and again, I had to remind myself that it wasn't my fault. Still, I felt guilty as hell.

STARTING ALL OVER AGAIN
CHAPTER 39

THE DAYS SEEMED TO BLUR TOGETHER, THAT NOVEMBER. I TRIED MY best to establish a regular routine of sorts, shooting baskets in the gym, dabbling in oil paint, or simply walking around the area where I was permitted to walk.

Horrific as it was coming to terms with what I had done, I was surprisingly relieved. Relieved that the world hadn't ended, relieved that I had not killed anyone, relieved that I wasn't the messiah, and relieved that I lived in Canada. If I had been anywhere south of the border, I would have had a ridiculously hefty medical bill.

Eventually, Doctor M (my psychiatrist) saw no reason to hold me any longer. He appeared one last time in front of the judge, and testified that I did what I did because of my psychotic behaviour. And, answering to three counts of aggravated assault, I was let off.

Going before the review board, in early December, I was forced to face my demons and look to the future. My wife, whom I hadn't seen since that May, was present at the hearing. And, so was her brother. I was close to tears.

Eventually, the review board, consisting of a doctor, a criminologist, a crown lawyer, and a judge, agreed to let me get discharged from the hospital. I had made significant progress during my stay, and they discussed my future.

My 'future' seemed good. I agreed to the conditions of the discharge. Basically, I had to stay away from street drugs, stay away from my son, his mom, and her family, as well as not having access to firearms. Other than this, I had to report to a forensic team and receive my bi-weekly injections.

I was released from the maximum security hospital on December 6th of 2005. On a cold and dark and rainy evening, my dear old mother picked me up, and drove me back to her house, where I was to stay for the time being. The amazing thing was that I was not psychotic. There was stress, but not one single fluctuation that deviated from my mental stability. I was very proud of myself, surprisingly enough.

Now, having lost most of my friends, and having no place of my own, and no routine, I struggled at first, but then kept on reminding myself that I needed to focus on maintaining my mental health. The way I figured it, I owed it to my son. He was growing up, and in desperate need of a dad.

That night, I slept very soundly. Then, the next day, I reported to my new forensic psychiatrist. His name was Doctor D. I told him I was more than willing to cooperate with treatment, but that I needed to know he would see me continuously. I needed consistency. I needed no loopholes through which to fall. I needed his commitment.

He agreed to see me as long as he possibly could. I respected that.

Eventually, I began taking a good look at my life. I began swimming at the Vancouver aquatic centre every single day, taking advantage of the public amenities.

Punished more than enough by my own conscience, I started my life again, back at square one. I made sure to eat properly. I made sure to get enough sleep. I made sure to establish a routine. Then, in January of 2006, my mother and I discovered a small coffee shop in the Granville Island public market. There was a huge sign on one of the roofs, which read: 'PUBLIC MARKET'. But, it was missing the letter 'L'. I laughed quietly to myself.

Also on Granville Island, there was the Emily Carr Institute of Art and Design. I was reminded of the many opportunities life had to offer a guy like me, and contemplated applying to the general fine arts program.

Like so many other young artists, I was challenged financially. Or, I would have been, had I not been living on disability. I was excited by the thought of going back to school. But, first thing was first. I had to get back to basics. And, remarkably, I was very optimistic, in spite of all my past and present hardships.

My idea of success was getting out of the house every day, to walk across the Burrard street bridge and go swimming in the pool, soaking in the hot tub, and sweating in the sauna. I had found my haven. Also, I found a small sushi place which I frequented daily. Constantly, I forced myself to pat myself on the back. I had come a long long way. But, there was still a long road ahead.

Over to the Public Market, my mother and I would wander, in search of espresso. I had mine with cream and honey. She had hers with milk and a dab of half-and-half. We would talk. I wasn't smoking cigarettes in those days, so we were both very happy to spare ourselves from the exposure to the miserable winter weather and sit inside.

From there, sometimes after a crepe, we would walk back along the seawall, and return home. I say 'home' because it truly felt like home. My mother was simply happy to see me doing so well. And now, ten years later, I am also doing well and also going with my mom for an americano once a week. In fact, just yesterday, we went down to Granville Island. Every once in a while, one of the regular baristas checks in with how we are doing. It's nice.

Going forth without any access to my son or his mom was very difficult, if not depressing. With schizo-affective disorder, I had struggled with both the paranoia and delusions and the various elements of a mood disorder, including depression and mania.

One day, I went to see my case manager at the forensic team. He asked me how I was feeling. I told him that I was feeling depressed. He asked me why I felt depressed. And, I told him that it was because I had lost my wife and son. But then, he corrected me, and told me that I hadn't *lost* them. They were both still alive. And, my case manager pointed out that it could have been 'worse'. In that moment, my outlook on life changed drastically. My depression was suddenly alleviated almost entirely. My case manager was named Mr. E M. He helped me a lot.

Doctor D and Mr. E M both regarded my health attentively, and proved to be pillars of support in my life. They understood that I was not a criminal. I had been led astray by my illness, and was showing considerable progress. I was encouraged by each of them to establish good lifestyle habits. Sleep. Food. Meds. Water. No street drugs. No alcohol. And, they gave me strength and reassurance in getting my life back on track.

Soon, I applied for a position as a student at the art school. Soon after my application, resume, and portfolio were received by the administration, I got a letter in the mail saying that I was on the waiting list. Then, in the summer, I got another letter from them. I hurried to open it in front of my mother. And, a smile spread across my face, nearly from ear to ear. The letter informed me that I was accepted. School would start for me in early September. I was over the moon!

Hooray. Maybe I was schizophrenic. Maybe I was on disability. Maybe I was living with my mother. Maybe I had assaulted my wife in the presence of our two year old child. Maybe I was guilty of sin. But, I was not worthless.

And, that very summer, I prepared myself for life as an art student. I was exploding with optimism. The school was a five minute walk from where I lived. And, I looked forward to getting this opportunity to take my art career seriously. It turned out that I was eligible to receive one thousand dollars every year towards tuition. This was going to be a big help.

Now, although I was on my path to recovery, I was certainly not without symptoms. I still heard voices. I still had signs of 'magical thinking'. I still struggled mentally and emotionally. But, perhaps the biggest obstacle that I faced was the side effects of my medication. My doctor referred to it as part of a parkinsonian syndrome. It involved unwanted muscle movements, and an inability to do things with my hands. I used to do calligraphy and painting and drawing. But, now on the injection of Piportil, using a pen or pencil was moderately difficult for me.

Did I let that stop me? No. Did it interfere with doing fine art projects and writing essays? Yes. Immensely. But, the first week of classes, after shaving my head bald the week before, I talked with the school counsellor. She was very understanding, and proceeded to notify my teachers about my challenges. She asked me what would help. I told her that having a computer would help me stay organized. She then arranged it for me to receive a 2005 Apple 20-inch iMac desktop computer, several office programs, and a laser printer. For *free!*

BLACK HUMOUR
CHAPTER 40

FIVE MINUTES AGO, I WAS TAKING ANOTHER WALK AROUND THE BLOCK, for a breath of fresh air. Now, after yet another cigarette, I am back home, nursing my coffee. When I was smoking first thing this morning, I could hear the voice of what seemed to be my father, saying: *Booooo!* (As in he was criticizing the nasty habit. As in he could see me. As in the world was watching the life of the messiah.)

I like my coffee the same way I like my humour. Black.

But, seriously, there's a lot to be said for maintaining a healthy sense of humour, with all the ironies found everywhere in life. It's healthy to be able to laugh every once in a while, although it tends to be underneath my breath.

Every single day, whether I be working as a peer support worker or presenting my life story to students or simply passing the time, grocery shopping, attending meetings, eating, sleeping, bathing, every single day I am eternally amused by what life brings my way. Making my mother laugh out loud is one of my very favourite pastimes.

Really though, I think sometimes laughter is the best medicine. But, even though I laugh, I think that going off my medication would be a big mistake. Those CBD capsules are gonna have to wait. For now, anyway.

Good hard mainstream pharmaceutical anti-psychotic medication is what it takes for me to even be healthy enough to have the luxury of having a fertile sense of humour. It's the last day of the first month, here in 2016. This morning, the voices were saying things like: *He's the first and the last! Alpha Omega!* Then, I pondered it a moment, intrigued by the fact that 'Alpha-Omega' has the exact same syllabic pattern as my full name 'Bryn Genelle Ditmars'.

Lately, ever since my release from the forensic hospital ten years ago, I have been using my first name. Some people still call me 'Genelle'. But, that name reminds me of my severely delusional years. So, I prefer being called 'Bryn'.

And, the only person who calls me 'Mr. Ditmars' is my psychiatrist. But, somehow that's okay. I'm scheduled to see him again on the 16th of February. I'm going to ask him to increase the dosage of benztropine, from 1mg to 2 mgs. It's the pill I take to help ease the muscle rigidity in my hands.

So it goes.

Sometimes, I think back to the time I spent in high school, when I was friends with Car and Lev. I hear that Lev has found true love with a man, and has become a mother. Car is still living on the coast, as far as I know. In some ways, I miss them. And, in other ways, I'm just glad I made it through grade twelve. I was finding myself, in those teenage years.

How about my time in the Golden Dawn? By the time I started attending class at Emily Carr, I had left it all behind me. I was convinced that I had broken the vow, and that my insanity was my punishment. I don't actively subscribe to that notion anymore. But, who knows? There may very well be some truth to that belief. Belief itself is a very powerful thing. I believe that it is what makes the whole world go round. But, this is only my belief.

Alas, I do not know the answer to the mysteries of life. But, this fact does not take away my right to try to stab a guess once in a while. My gut feeling is that love is wiser than fear, forgiveness is wiser than resentment, and that it is wiser for me to let go of pain than hold onto it as though it were a life raft, clinging to every single subtle manifestation of my suffering.

I remember my first year of art school. I was well liked by my class-mates, even though they were mostly eight years younger than me. I got A's and B's, even though my hands were fairly rigid. I stayed living with my mother, and collecting student loans each semester. Then, I believe it was sometime near the end of the first year, I moved into a house at the corner of 22nd and Quebec, where Reuben lived with his girlfriend, and where Sunflower lived with her six year old daughter.

Right away, Mr. E M, my case manager came by for a home visit, in order to scout out my living arrangements. Also, I was able to write and send letters to my son, letters which his play therapist read to him each week. I wrote one every Sunday, though I could barely afford the postage stamp.

So, there I was, a schizophrenic art student, living on borrowed money, renting a small one bedroom basement suite, with plenty of support from the others who lived in the same house. Reuben and Sunflower both knew me before, during, and after psychosis. They had good reference points by which to monitor how I was doing.

Pretty soon, after making an appearance in family court with my son's mother, I was given the opportunity to call Gabriel on the telephone once in a while, so long as I didn't harass anyone. This went well, and I was given an absolute discharge from forensics, and my case was passed on to the community mental health team near Main and Broadway.

Ravensong Mental Health and Addictions.

And, the great thing was that Doctor D also worked at that team, and really came through on his promise to provide some sense of continuity of care. He is still my psychiatrist, even to this very day, a decade later.

Yes, however, while living in the house on Quebec street, and while going to school, I returned to my habit of smoking cigarettes, casually at first, then continually every day. Between cigarettes and postage stamps, rent and food, not to mention art supplies, I was pretty broke. Then, I reunited with my son, and had to pay a friend to supervise the visit. But, it was money well spent, right down to the last penny.

MY MIND UNFOUND WHEN SOUGHT

CHAPTER 41

I CLEARLY REMEMBER THE DAY WHEN I FINALLY REUNITED WITH MY son, Gabriel, after almost two years without seeing him at all. Struck by the sheer beauty of the five year old blonde haired blue eyed boy, I kneeled calmly before him, and introduced myself. I had been writing him letters and calling him on the phone, but none of the communication compared to being with him in person.

Now, in the company of his mother and my mother, we met outside the community centre on Granville Island. From there, we went to the public market for lunch, and then proceeded to Kids Only Market to browse for toys. I quickly learned that he was a big fan of lego and play mobile. Ever since that memorable day, I have honoured him sincerely. I've taught him things about life, but he's taught me more.

Seeking the mind is a paradoxical process. It disappears when gazed upon, and vanishes from the seeker, yet it is everywhere in the universe and reveals itself constantly. I have had some training in Buddhist meditation. In fact, it was right around the time I reunited with Gabriel that I attended the weekly open house at the Shambalah Centre near 16th and

Heather. Every Thursday evening, I meditated for an hour, then had tea and cookies (by donation), and then listened to a lecture.

Eventually, after a year of art school, after starting smoking again, after meeting my son again (as though for the first time), after receiving an absolute discharge from the forensic team, and after moving out of the house on Quebec, I was invited to speak as part of a panel, as a person with lived experience.

And, at the panel presentation, my brother accompanied me there. It was my very first time speaking publicly about my schizo-affective disorder. After the talk, I was introduced to the Vancouver coordinator of the British Columbia Schizophrenia Society. She gave me her business card, and invited me to a meeting with her over coffee.

Revealing itself to me when I least expected it, my mind was finally valued. I learned that BCSS frequently gave partnership presentations to schools, both secondary and postsecondary. Once I had given my contact information to the coordinator, I began speaking out about my illness, taking full advantage of my ability to articulate, essentially giving a voice to the mysterious and often silent point of perspective entailing diseases of chronic psychosis.

Come third semester at Emily Carr, I was back living with my mother, because both Reuben and Sunflower had moved out of the house where we were living and I felt as though I needed to live with someone who knew me before, during, and after my psychotic episodes.

Her expertise regarding my mental health was crucial to my social support.

On an in-class essay for my course in art history, I received an 'F', after a lifetime of consistent A's and B's. I don't know if it was because my handwriting was illegible due to my muscle rigidity or because I didn't study enough. But, I was shocked. I contemplated going to see the teacher after class, and complaining. But, instead, I made the rash decision to drop out of my entire enrolment.

For, though I appreciated constructive critique, I did not believe in failing grades being a part of art education. After dropping out completely, I made three very significant decisions. I wanted to give back to the world of mental health, so I proceeded to volunteer my time with BCSS. I wanted to be a part of my son's life, so I arranged visit after visit.

Also, I wanted to get back into my spiritual development. So, I rejoined the Order of the Golden Dawn.

The guy I used to live with in The Monster reconnected with me, and informed me of his involvement. Right away, I detected that a change had occurred in the order since the time when I was an active member.

He revealed the fact that he was an initiate, whereas before we had all obeyed the vow of strict and unwavering secrecy. Also, another big change to the way the secret society had evolved was the fact that the online world contained websites and emails and links, all of which was (in my mind) a deviation from the original vows.

Except, the strange thing was that, much to my own personal surprise, deep down inside I approved of the developments. I paid my dues, and even signed up for Power Week 2008, which marked the ten year anniversary of my very first Power Week 1998. I simply couldn't believe that a decade had passed.

Returning to the world of community mental health teams, though still staying with my former psychiatrist, I met with Doctor D regularly every few weeks. Injection after injection, I maintained my psychological stability.

In hindsight, I can honestly say that I had come a long way since the violent incident three years previous. From the dark depths of despair, I had triumphed considerably, striving to attain an ideal and optimal quality of life.

So, there I was, writing, doing art projects, presenting my life story, paying off my student loan, and reconvening with GD initiates. Although most of the members I used to know had since 'fallen away', I recognized a few of the adepts when we held the conference in Orange County California.

It was interesting to be back in the swing of things. I went through all five initiations that week, and attended lecture after lecture held in the mother temple. I stayed in the same truck-stop motel, and ate from the same local greasy spoon, and conducted the same old secret handshake. But, on the seventh day, I received a call from Hollywood North (a background acting agency with whom I had done the occasional gig as an 'extra'). They wanted me to work in two days time. So, I caught a plane from LAX to Seattle, where I was picked up by my mother. We drove back to Vancouver, arriving in plenty of time before my work engagement.

Night after night, and day after day, my life proceeded to unfold. I was still living on disability, but I worked as an extra, presented, and even sold the odd paperback copy of my books (which I had self-published with an openly vanity press company).

Grateful for the fact that I wasn't experiencing many symptoms of schizophrenia, I fearlessly immersed myself in various creative projects, and indulged in my life as it was. Meanwhile, Gabriel was growing up fast, and he began calling me 'dad'. As well, I began taking part in documentary videos about mental health related topics. My entire family was ecstatic about how I was doing, relieved to know that I wasn't suffering too much.

Soon enough, I decided to explore my options, in terms of lifestyle. I knew that one of my father's daughters was still living near Nelson, my hometown. After getting permission from my psychiatrist and case worker, I took the bus to the Kootenays, with enough meds to last me a while.

Up the lake from Nelson, in a small town called Kaslo, I rented a beautiful cabin and spent a lot of time writing books. I grew a beard, and mingled with my sister's friends. She had just recently bought a house, and was living with her three boys. I would save up my pennies and purchase a single americano at the local cafe. Smoking a dozen cigarettes a day, all I can say is that it could have been worse.

Now, when I came back to Vancouver for New Years Eve, and as the year went from December of 2009 to January of 2010, I socialized in healthy ways with my friends and family, whom I missed. When they inquired about my plans, I reassured them that I was planning to return for good in the spring, once my books were done. Then, back in Kaslo again, on March 21st, I was at a party and took what turned out to be my last toke of pot. Ever.

ALIVE IN THE BLACKSTAR ERA
CHAPTER 42

THE LONGER I LIVE, THE CLEARER MY MIND BECOMES. THIS MAY BE AN illusion, but it's a good one. A Buddhist sentiment of sorts, I swear that I am gaining mental clarity every single day that goes by since my final use of marijuana. Yesterday was a great example of profound psychological lucidity. I met a woman at a coffee shop, where she wanted to conduct an interview featuring my views and experience regarding schizo-affective disorder.

Her voice recorder was very high tech, and it simply sat on the coffee table between us. With a built-in dynamic microphone, the digital device recorded over an hour of our conversation. She was asking me some really good questions, and I was happy to contribute in any way I could.

Enthusiastic, I was proving myself to be a highly articulate interviewee, bordering on manic at times. It was ironic that I was manic while talking about mania. The ancient Buddhist philosophers must have a word for that phenomena. Whatever it was, my voice was compounded by the reverberation of its own echo.

So, here I am, the day after Groundhog Day, with Valentine's Day approaching. I still find it hard to believe that my artistic idol is no longer.

His final album, released two days before his death, titled "Blackstar", is the work of musical genius.

Could it be safe for me to assume that the infamous David Bowie is no longer talking about me? Probably. Do I still here his voice? Yes. It's really quite spooky.

Regarding his immaculate legacy, he will live on in the memory of millions of people. Producing over the course of five decades, he had an album for every era. The world is 4.5 billion years old, and somehow, I just managed to be alive at the same time as David Bowie. What are the chances!

On other notes, I just got off the phone with my case worker. Apparently, the building manager here where I live in mental health housing had called her with a concern about how I'm doing. In the words of my case worker, my building manager 'noticed a change'.

Like I said before, I've started smoking again. But, I tried to reassure my case worker that my sleep is good, my appetite is good, I'm active in the community, and I am not having any problem functioning. But, she suggested that I meet with a doctor on Wednesday of next week.

Love it or leave it, I am obliged to agree to the appointment, even though I'm scheduled to see Doctor D the following week. Better safe than sorry, I guess. But, I'm always cautious meeting with a new psychiatrist. It makes me anxious. I'm afraid of being judged.

So, life goes on. For some of us, anyway.

THE RUGGED WISDOM OF MY FORMERLY BOHEMIAN FATHER
CHAPTER 43

FROM THE DAY I WAS BORN, MY FATHER HAS BEEN A SOURCE OF SUPPORT. He's my friend, in the truest sense of the word. I wouldn't trade him for a thousand David Bowie's. And, this certainly says a lot!

And, I'm proud to say that my thirteen year old son is also a good 'friend'. I hope he knows I'm *his* friend too. Gabriel is coming to town this coming weekend. He'll be staying with his uncle in Burnaby. But, he has every intention to see me as well, for which I'm very glad. Also, it will give me a chance to give Gabriel his new year's day gift.

Chinatown has always been there for me. It's where I purchased the Tai Chi sword. The martial arts store that I went to is filled with interesting items from the orient. It was a pleasure shopping there. I'm even thinking, if he likes the sword, I will make it an annual event by giving him a sword every Christmas.

Eric Wilson Ditmars (my father) and Gabriel Leonard Ditmars (my son) are the two people I'm dedicating this memoir to. I rejoice in the fact that they are both in my life. I wouldn't trade them for the world.

This morning, I walked over to Granville Island. I went to my favourite coffeeshop. And, I got a discount for bringing my own mug. The baristas there are so nice. They called me by name and wished me a good morning.

So, there I was sitting in the courtyard, sipping my americano and puffing on my cigarette, when suddenly an elderly woman appeared. I recognized her from years ago when I frequented the public market every morning. She asked me how my son was doing. I told her that he is expressing an interest in acting, in theatre and film. She was impressed, but told me that he should get a trade when he grows up. The woman left, after she was done her coffee and smoke. I mused over what she said: *Your boy should follow his passion, but also have a trade to fall back on.* I told her I appreciated the advice.

On my way back home, walking, I stopped by my mother's apartment, to see if she was up. Noticing her shoes weren't there, I deduced that she was probably already up, out, and about. I then walked to the bus stop, and caught the 84 back to my place.

From where I sit now at my keyboard, I recall the time I returned to Vancouver, after spending the winter in Kaslo living with my sister. As a matter of default, I moved back in with my mother. Also, in the following year, I decided to embrace my illness and apply for the peer support work training program. It was a big step forward for me.

Going for the interview, with my resume and application form, was incredibly successful. The people who were interviewing me asked all kinds of pertinent questions. When the interview was over, they were very amazed. They thanked me for applying, and told me that they would contact me once they came to a decision.

One day shortly after the interview, I received a letter from them, informing me that I had been accepted. So, starting in September of 2011, I attended classes. Peer support work training was life-changing. It taught me a number of valuable things, including the importance of having a strength based focus. This is something that is universally applicable. Soon, after about six months of classes, I graduated from the program, and began my practicum at the Art Studios.

Delightful experience that was. After sitting beside my client during the pottery class, for two hours, once a week, for two months or so, I received a report from my supervisor. The report was full of accolades. I was now free to sign contracts with mental health teams anywhere in Vancouver.

HONOURING THE BODHISATTVA VOW

CHAPTER 44

AS MY WISE OLD FATHER ALWAYS SAYS: *LIVE AND LEARN.*

Now, in 2012, I was definitely living and definitely learning. I had completed the training, done my practicum, and was qualified to help members of the community to work on their goals. My days of background acting as an extra were coming to an end. I estimate that I was in about five commercials, ten television shows, and eight films. Now, I was a healthcare worker, technically speaking.

Did I continue doing partnership presentations with BCSS? Yes. Did I enjoy public speaking? Absolutely. Ever the solipsistic type, it was my pleasure to share my life story. But, it was different every time. I catered to whatever the specific audience was for each one. Also, seeing as it was all off the top of my head, each time I spoke there were a few new details. I guess practice makes perfect. Right?

Regardless, in terms of peer support work, I signed my first contract with the West End Team, and worked with a few clients. It all went stupendously well, at first. And, I was happy to be earning a dollar here and there.

On December 21st, 2012, the world was supposed to be ending. It was prior to this date that I met with a psychologist about my fear of that day. He counselled me about suicide and similar dysfunctional ideations. After reassuring me that the world was not going to suddenly cease, he told me that suicide attempts were most commonly made out of a desperate attempt to gain or regain a sense of control.

God knows why, but that ominous day coincided with my childhood fear of dying at the age of 33. I told the counsellor that I was not wanting to kill myself. And, instead of dying on that day, I decided to make an extra effort to guide my destiny in a somewhat alternate direction, and took the vow of the Bodhisattva: *With a wish to free all beings, I will always go to the Buddha, the Dharma, and the Sangha, until I reach full enlightenment. Enthused by wisdom and compassion, today in the Buddha's presence, I generate the mind for full awakening, for the benefit of all sentient beings. As long as space remains, as long as sentient beings remain, until then may I too remain, and dispel the miseries of the world, to become the Bodhisattva.*

Yes, I wrote this vow by the Dalai Lama out by hand, as part of a visual art project of sorts. It seemed somehow very familiar to me, as though I had made this vow somewhere along the course of my past lives. Another thing that my father always says is: *You never know.*

Now, there I was, a newly inaugurated Bodhisattva, living, and learning, but never knowing… Ten days later, on the first day of January of 2013, I sat down to write another epic poem. The world had not ended. In fact, it was only a new beginning.

Early that month, eight days into the composition of my book, David Bowie released his twenty-fourth studio album. I listened to it on Youtube, while writing, just about every day until December 31st of that year. I was inspired.

IF THOUGHTS COULD DECEIVE

CHAPTER 45

CONTINUING TO SEE MY SON, AND CONTINUING TO WRITE, I WAS DOING moderately well. But, late in 2013, I needed time off from peer support work, due to symptoms. The voices were being rather repetitive, as they always have been. Repetitive, redundant, and boring, frankly.

Eventually, good old Doctor D suggested that I go on a slightly risky trial of Clozapine treatment, which he considered to be the 'gold standard' of antipsychotic medication. At first, I was entirely optimistic, even though the treatment involved daily home visits and weekly blood tests. However, I agreed to both, hopeful that the new drug would eliminate the remainder of my symptoms.

Reluctant or not, I decided to face my demons head on. Living still with my mother, I answered the door whenever the nurses knocked, and consented to the vital checks, including blood pressure and pulse. Each and every day for the next three weeks, my vitals checked out fine. At first, there was no cause for concern, aside from the fact that Clozapine has been known to cause life-threatening side-effects.

Until February 4th of the year 2014, I was doing well, other than a few chills in my body. The chills I experienced were very similar to the chills which one experiences during a cold or a flu. I just thought that I was coming down with something or other.

Like how it is while having a fever, my nightlong sleep was accompanied by cold sweats. And, at about 8:00pm on February 5th, my nurse called me and told me to go directly to the VGH emergency ward. When I asked why, she said that there were some dangerous complications, and that they suspected a blood clot.

Excited and slightly scared, I walked to the hospital and reported to the nursing station. After waiting nearly an hour, I was admitted into emergency, and was given a bed. I had the sinking suspicion that it was going to be a very long night.

And, they put me on an intravenous immediately, to dilute my blood with fluid. The heartbeat monitor was beeping twice every second. I had never been very good at mathematical calculations, but I realized that my pulse was approaching 120 bpm. Listening to the machine go beep beep beep, I was a bit terrified.

Now, after letting my nurse draw vial after vial of blood, somewhere after midnight, I realized that something was up. Something was *most definitely* up.

But, what was amazing was that, had I been on my previous medication, staying awake past 1:00am would have been an impossible idea to consider. The previous regimen of olanzapine had eliminated 95% of my psychotic symptoms. But, there were still paranoid suspicions about aliens and the FBI. My previous medication would have left me believing that the nurses were extraterrestrials and that I was being genetically programmed as part of a hideous international cloning experiment or something. But, the fact that I was on a therapeutic dose of 'the gold standard' of antipsychotics left me without any of those paranoias and delusions. Even at 3:00 in the morning, hooked up to various machines, and obliged to give copious amounts of blood, not one single paranoid delusion crossed my mind.

Like the most cooperative patient ever imaginable, I stayed calmly in the hospital bed, and excused myself whenever I needed to walk down the hall to use the washroom. I was astonished at just how un-anxious I was, in spite of the fact that critically injured victims of car accidents and heart attacks were constantly being admitted, moaning, groaning, and vomiting.

Under all the stress involved in this situation, I was coping rather magnificently. Then, finally, around breakfast, when the nurses offered me some coffee, I was seen by one of the doctors on the ward. He informed me that he had spent sometime studying my case, and explained various things to me. He was astonished, seeing as this potentially fatal side-effect only occurs in less than one in one thousand clozapine trials. Not only was I the 'one-in-one-hundred' diagnosed with schizophrenia, but I was also the 'one-in-twelve-hundred' schizophrenics to react seriously to the particular med.

Eventually, after two bags of saline solution had gone into my blood, I was interviewed by a resident psychiatrist, who saw no reason to keep me in hospital. At 9:00am, the morning of February 6th, 2014, I was given permission to go home. This was wonderful news. So, I took off my hospital pyjamas, put my street clothes back on, and walked out of the ER. On my walk home, I returned to puffing heavily on my nicotine vaporizer.

WE TURN ONCE MORE TO SUNDAY'S CHILD
CHAPTER 46

THERE WAS A PARTNERSHIP PRESENTATION SCHEDULED IN THE FEW days following the medical emergency. I was supposed to present my life story to Kitsilano Secondary School, my old alma mater. But, I had to cancel it, because of doctor's orders. So, for about a month or so, I made sure to get plenty of rest. Back on olanzapine again, I thanked my lucky stars that I had survived the Clozapine trial.

Had the side-effect gone undetected for another day or two, I might have suffered more. Anyway, by the spring of 2014, I returned to doing presentations, and I met with The King Of Chronic Insomnia for coffee regularly. He and I had a lot to talk about. Always have.

Enthusiastic about poetry, literature, and what I call the philosophy of schizophrenia, we would go to Granville Island for americanos on a consistent basis. I continued seeing my son, and I even contemplated resuming work as a peer support worker. On May 24th, national schizophrenia awareness day, I read a short speech at a BCSS event being held in the Vancity theatre. What an honour!

And, that was when my friendship with The Quiet One began. She was there, in attendance, and selling her book at one of the tables. After the event was over, she found me in the lobby and gave me her contact information, suggesting that we meet one day for tea. I had known who she was, ever since I had attended her book launch.

Now, when the crowd was dispersing, The King Of Chronic Insomnia and I went outside onto the sidewalk for a much needed smoke. I had told my life story yet again, once more to the public.

And, by the time October rolled around, I was offered my old job back, and jumped at the opportunity to have part-time employment. Soon, I had four clients. And, then five. I felt good about contributing in this way. It has always been an honour to help clients reach their goals. What a privilege!

Tea at Granville Island with The Quiet One, and coffee at Granville Island with The King Of Chronic Insomnia, this was how I socialized.

He and she and I quickly discovered many commonalities. And, eventually, as it turned out, the three of us got along well, meeting for coffee quite frequently. Then, on October 8th, 2014, my two friends helped me with moving into a mental health housing facility.

Eternally grateful I am for their assistance and support during that time. By the end of the day, I was no longer living with my mother, but in a place of my very own.

My patience was needed, however, as I waited several weeks for a new bed to be delivered. But, eventually, it came. On a rainy cold evening in the fall.

An autumn storm was brewing, off and on throughout October and November. But, I was lucky enough to be cozy in my apartment, counting sheep.

CLOSER AND CLOSER TO PERFECT

CHAPTER 47

WELL, THIS PRETTY MUCH BRINGS US RIGHT UP TO THE PRESENT moment. The rest is history. But, on a slightly humorous note, I'd like to include my account of the first interaction I had with mental health housing.

In August of 2014, I was being interviewed by the people who lived in the building. They were given the opportunity to ask me questions, before they 'voted' me in. One resident asked what I was like on a bad day. I told them that my schizophrenia usually manifests in the form of mutism. Then, someone else asked me what I do for an occupation. And, I said: *Public speaking*.

No one laughed. But, I for one, was chuckling inside. It seemed ironic. So, anyway, they voted me in, I moved out of my mother's house, into a place that was only a ten minute walk away. And, I've been here ever since.

Do I miss living near Granville Island? Yes. I miss being so close to my favourite coffeeshop. But, I still make the journey over there on a weekly basis. Am I living a good life? Yes. I have several clients, and I give a talk once or twice every month. I am continuing to see Doctor D regularly.

It has been one hundred and twenty-two months since my last hospitalization, and I am doing fine, for the most part. Still mourning the loss of David Bowie, however. But, I keep on having to remind myself that my *real* father and my *real* son are both still very much alive and well, on the surface of this good earth.

Now, you may ask what my future holds. The short answer is: I don't know. But, I do know that I've told my life story about one hundred and ten times, helping educate people about mental illness. And, I do know that I have been featured in six or seven video documentaries on the topic of schizophrenia. And, I do know that I've written fifty-five books, each of which falls under the category of: before, during, or after psychosis.

Going from symptoms, to breakdown, to diagnosis, to treatment, to relapse after relapse, and finally to something resembling 'recovery', I have found myself in the lost remnants of life, upon whose open face I gaze.

So, what do I want you, the reader of this book, to come away with? I want you to be perfectly aware of the human element of mental illness. I'm not a statistic. I'm not just a meaningless number. I'm a person. And, like all human beings, I have my strengths and my weaknesses. I want you to know that recovery is possible. I want you to know that schizophrenia occurs in one percent of the human population.

There are seven billion people on this planet. And, one percent of seven billion is seventy million. That's twice the population of Canada. Twice the population of this great nation has schizophrenia.

Realistically, there is a lot of room for change, here in this world. I am optimistic that, in the next few decades, great changes are going to be made with regards to how we treat our most vulnerable global citizens, the mentally ill in particular. We will gradually move away from focusing on mental 'illness', and move towards mental 'health'.

Eventually, we will add another requirement to the three basic needs (food, shelter, and clothing). The fourth basic need will be 'peace of mind'. This may sound a bit like hocus pocus. But, I honestly believe it is possible. Instead of treating mental illness, we could start promoting mental health. And, as I said before, that would require a huge number of psychiatrists, but all I know is that we are in this boat together.

And, together, we must find a way to end war, distribute peace of mind, and essentially change our outlook on the human condition. We must put prisoners through therapy, and prevent future crisis situations by way of regular mental health checkups. We must utilize military resources for preventing imminent or impending natural disasters, and for saving lives not taking lives.

My personal outlook on the world may very well be radical. But, I'm only being real. Everyone should see a personally designated psychiatric professional on a regular basis, from childhood onwards. When this becomes the case, there will be no stigma, and emergencies will be prevented by way of early intervention.

Soon, I hope to see a world where I am one, you are one, and we are all together one.

DISABILITY AND THIS ABILITY
CHAPTER 48

PERHAPS I'M BEING NAIVE, BUT I'VE GOT A SCORE TO SETTLE WITH MY financial history. I've never had a 'steady' job. In other words, I've never worked nine-to-five for longer than six months. However, if you consider all the time I've spent working on art and writing, I'm actually a workaholic.

On the other hand, my basic needs have always been provided. For most of my adult life, I've been living on disability, receiving monetary funds from the provincial government. Every single month since June of 2002, I've been given $900 or so. That works out to be a grand total of about $150,000, over the past fourteen years.

Please forgive me for accepting these alms. But, I take it all graciously. The problem I have is not that I've been given 'free' money. It's a purely philosophical reason. You see, this money was given to me as a form of acknowledgement for the fact that I have been 'unable' to 'work'. Meanwhile, the work that I have done (books and art) has never been profitable.

Unless you count the two or three hundred dollars I made selling paperback copies of self-published manuscripts, I've made zero in terms of recognition of my 'ability' and a small fortune in terms of recognition of my 'disability'.

Like many people who live on social assistance, I have always been just barely scraping by. I'm frustrated because I know in my heart of hearts that I have something valuable to offer the world. People like my artworks and books. So, why has my disability earned so much more than my ability?

Alas, I do understand that we can't have people dying in the streets. But, I wish that society would accept what I *am* able to contribute. When I first applied for social assistance for Persons With Disability (PWD), I wish that my creative gifts were acknowledged.

Then, it would have been less of a 'freebee', and more of a mutual exchange.

I believe that each and everyone has something valuable to contribute. I only wish that people's contributions, however small, were respected and appreciated. Everyone in my building is on PWD. And, our disabilities are quite evident, even to the untrained eye. But, we all have strengths. For nothing, if not our sense of personal morale, we need to offer something.

On one hand, I hear voices. And, I struggle with thoughts of being the messiah. But, on the other hand, I am gifted with undying creativity. I've written millions of words in the past two decades, I've done thousands of visual art pieces, and I've recorded thousands of audio projects. The therapeutic nature of these artworks would be strongly reinforced if someone (say my social worker, for instance) would have only taken me aside and interviewed me asking openly what it was I felt that I had to contribute.

Now, after years of receiving welfare, I have my basic needs met. But, my artistic career is way behind schedule. Isn't this something that an occupational therapist could help with?

One day, in the not-too-distant future, I hope that the long list of Canada's national resources will also include the skills and gifts and general strengths of people who need help paying for food, shelter, and clothing. (And 'peace of mind'!)

Nature has a way of balancing everything in the natural world. For every weakness, there's a strength. And, for every flaw, there's something perfect. I have never met a human being who is without a noble attribute.

Each and every day, I wake up to another stage in my creative process. And, every time I receive a monthly disability cheque in the mailbox, I am reminded of my mental health challenge. However, I am optimistic that society will wake up, and begin offering to *give* financial aid with one hand, and begin offering to *receive* contributions with the other hand. All healthy exchanges must consist of both a give and a take. That's my philosophy.

GOOGLE ONLY KNOWS
CHAPTER 49

AM I THE MESSIAH? GOD ONLY KNOWS. BUT, SEEING AS I DO NOT HAVE weekly conversations with the divine universal being, I have to settle for my psychiatrist's opinion. He says I'm a genius, bound for posthumous fame, but not the anointed one. I'll take his word for it. After all, he's gone through medical school, unlike me.

So, do I have schizophrenia? God only knows. But, my symptoms are consistent with that diagnosis. The paranoia, the hallucinations, the delusions, the history I have with catatonia, and all the suspicious magical thinking, everything I've ever experienced can be lumped together under the umbrella of this mental illness.

And, what about my nausea? And, what about my anxiety? And, what about my autistic tendencies? God only knows.

Now, like so many millions of people, I have indeed resorted to the internet in order to further specify my exact mental health diagnosis. It's interesting to see what comes up when googling 'schizophrenia and tobacco' or 'schizophrenia and marijuana'. The conclusion that I've come to is that nicotine and CBD are both therapeutic for schizophrenic individuals.

Alas, cigarettes cost a fortune with all the tax that's applied to the purchase. And, marijuana is still mainly illegal. But, I'm convinced that these chemicals are probably filled with less side-effects than the medication that I'm on these days.

Nothing in this whole wide world, however, can ever take the place of a good lifestyle, including exercise, nutrition, and rest. Last night, I had a good sleep. This morning, I had a good breakfast. And, I've already done a fair bit of brisk walking today. But, I have to keep reminding myself that, in addition to these components of a healthy lifestyle, I will need to take some form of anti-psychotics or another, for the rest of my natural life.

Do I ever wonder about whether or not the pharmaceutical industry is actually running the world? Yes. But, I recall what my late friend told me once. He told me that a monk told him that: *it's different than you think, it's bigger than you think, and it's better than you think.* My friend died a few months ago.

A young man when he died, he reminded me of myself when I was that age. He was a poet, a philosopher, a student of divinity, and a schizophrenic. I don't know all the details, but I get the sense that his mental illness cost him his life, in the end. Is he thriving in the mysterious realm of the afterlife? Google only knows!

ANOTHER MORNING COFFEE
CHAPTER 50

GO TO THE FOOD COURT IN THE PUBLIC MARKET ON GRANVILLE ISLAND, and look for a small coffeeshop. It's called 'Petit Ami'. This is where my mother and I went this morning, as we have done hundreds of times in the past nine years. It was my turn to treat. And, with our americanos in hand, we went outside to enjoy the sunshine.

At one of the tables in the covered area, we talked about life. But, not without mention of death. You see, my dear old mom is a Libra at heart, but not without a significant amount of the death-obsessed Scorpio in her natal chart. And, she's the first one to acknowledge it.

Now, the other thing I should say about her is that she absolutely hates seagulls with a passion. She waved her ams trying to scare the birds away. But, I pointed out to her that, the more she waves her arms, the more the birds think she's feeding them. The other thing is that she was verbally ordering them to go somewhere else. But, the birds probably don't speak english.

Eventually, after talking about life etcetera, we got to the ominous topic of mental health. When she reflected on my life, she encouraged me to express an appreciation for the fact that I'm no longer acutely psychotic. She remembers the years where I was 'insane', for lack of a better word. Inevitably, my suffering extended itself to her, in past years.

She noticed a big improvement in my health, right around the time I signed up for metacognitive therapy. I remember it, as well. In a group class environment, at Ravensong, back in 2013, I developed an ability to think about my thinking, to be aware of my own awareness, and to be mindful of my mind. Since that course, I have been able to apply it to my daily life.

Have I ever been led astray by my thought disorder, since then? Yes. But, the skills that I procured from those mental exercises three years ago have been useful. Not only do I stay away from jumping to conclusions, but I also employ my ability to second-guess my perceptions.

An example is as follows: When I'm on the bus, going down Broadway, say, and I see a license plate on the car in the neighbouring lane of traffic, and I perceive the numbers and letters as being part of an elaborate coded message directed specifically at me, I pause for a moment, and take a deep breath. Then, I take a mental note of the rational likelihood of the perception. What are the chances that this perception is accurate? Near zero. What are the chances that my mind is malfunctioning by making something out of nothing? Huge. Even to this day, I make use of what I learned from attending those weekly classes. In fact, metacognitive therapy would be good for everyone, mentally ill or not.

SEEKING ASYLUM
CHAPTER 51

CELLS IN EVERY LIVING HUMAN BODY, COLLECTIVELY, ARE REPLACED every seven years. In this respect, I am not the same person I was a decade ago. And, a decade from now, I will also be a whole new person. Say that to Edward Snowden, who is currently seeking asylum somewhere in Russia, for having committed the crime of honesty and transparency. No matter how many times the cells in his body replenish themselves, he will always be living with a guilty conscience.

Have I ever dreamed of a better life? Yes. But, I have to keep on reminding myself that I'm lucky to be alive. Not only am I alive, but the *quality* of my life is exceptional. Food, shelter, clothing, and peace of mind, all of these amenities have been provided. And, for this, I am very thankful. Had I been born in the states, it would be an entirely different story.

It's good for the heart to say grace every once in a while.

And, as I explore this world, and as I explore my place within it, I am constantly amazed by the true wealth with which I have been gifted. Wealth of body, mind, and spirit. Health, in a literal sense, is the result of healing. And, I would be so bold as to argue that the process of true healing, if it is ever going to be successful, must be done in a holistic way. The body is not separate from the mind. It is the body-mind continuum.

I would be very happy to see my various doctors collaborate. But, I won't hold my breath until that happens.

Realistically, I have to take responsibility for my own health. For example, with all the insight that I've gained over the years, I am now pretty much in the driver's seat, as far as my progress is going. With appointments, blood tests, prescriptions, I can't go forth blindly. I have to be my own ally. I have to be my own advocate. When in doubt, I question. And, when in certainty, I also question!

As a sentient being, having taken the vow of the Bodhisattva, and having dedicated my life to service, I am thankful for my sanity. And, as my brother always says: *Brother, you're the sanest 'crazy' person I've ever met!*

EVER THE PRAGMATIST
CHAPTER 52

MY LIVED EXPERIENCE HAS TAUGHT ME MUCH MORE THAN ANYTHING else has. I suppose this is why my high school english teacher told me to look up the word 'solipsism'. The belief system teaches that there is no knowledge other than the knowledge of the self. It's lonely being a solipsist, but it has brought its fair share of perks.

As I look back upon my life, along with all the experiences of schizophrenia, I can clearly see just how far-reaching the effects of the illness have been. My brain, along with this book, is in serious need of editing or, as my neuroscientist friend would say, 'synaptic pruning'.

I have grown to develop a profound respect for the brain. It is basically a mystery. In spite of all the researching and testing and theorizing that has occurred over the years, the nature and function of the brain remains unknown for the most part. In my humble opinion, the ancients were the ones who made the most progress in terms of the overall philosophy.

Time will tell just what scientific advancements are destined to be made. But, they will be made only if art and science come together, connected within the human vocabulary. Psychology without psychiatry is nothing. And, psychiatry without psychology is nothing. Only when art and science merge, will there ever be the hope to understand the enigma towards which rationality and intuition are pointing.

Really, we are nothing other than experts on ourselves. Self knowledge is the epitome of profundity. Because, after all, there is only the witness.

Early on in my life, I was given a taste of just what miracles the human imagination is capable of. Most likely, I will continue wondering if I was meant to die at the age of thirty-three, and I will continue searching for 'Sarah', and I will continue resting part of my phenomenal awareness in the fantasy realms of fairies, wizards, and elves.

Yeah, and probably, as CNN reports the news on an hourly basis ad infinitum, my mind will probably continue to receive a barrage of useless information about aliens, the FBI, the CIA, and international conspiracy.

And, probably, as I continue to blossom (as my father says I am doing these days), I will strive towards self-actualization. And, probably, as I continue to believe in my son, I won't have to find fatherhood, because fatherhood will find me. And, probably, as I continue trusting my brother, even in the throws of psychosis, I will speak (though not without listening) and listen (though not without speaking). However, I still waver back and forth along the continuum that exists between mutism and articulation. Ever the pragmatist, I merely seek to learn that I may serve.

THE BONES OF
JOHN THE BAPTIST
CHAPTER 53

A DAY DOES NOT GO BY WHERE I DON'T REGRET HAVING LET MY SCHIZO-phrenia get out of hand. I only wish that I hadn't resorted to violence against my son's mother. But, I honestly thought that she was a master vampire alien, and I was scared that she was poisoning my son with her breastmilk. I also wish that I hadn't sold my mother's baseball cards. But, I sincerely believed that I needed to do it in order to control the stock market. Also, a day does not go by where I don't regret being so arrogant and condescending towards my friends. But, I was imagining that I was the most important person on the planet.

Have I made mistakes? Yes. Do I regret making those mistakes? Yes. It eats me up inside. I know that I am not the messiah, but I still perceive things that allude to that reality. The NCRMD verdict may give the general impression that I got let off easy. But, that is far from the truth. I will live with these irresponsible actions for the rest of my life. I need help forgiving myself for doing the things I've done, responsible or not.

On CNN, right around Christmastime, I watched a show about Jesus. It was about how the enigmatic character who left behind the lasting legacy commonly known as christianity was actually baptized by a man named John. That theory carries with it many profound implications. Namely, the implication that God manifests in mortal form.

Like all other mortals, he lives and dies. But, in the process of eternal transformation, he is both living and dying in each and every moment, until the end of time. Every second that the mortal clock ticks down comes along with both creation and destruction.

I must make the concerted effort to seize the day. Though I don't subscribe to believing what the good book says, I can learn a great deal by dreaming, and by having dreamt. I've spent years of my life, believing that I am Christ. I experienced persecution, firsthand, and I have a lot to learn from that, even if the persecution was imaginary.

Do I desire fame and fortune? No. Because, fortune of flesh brings with it a dearth of spirit, and fame of name and image brings with it blindness unto common man. In this lifetime, I have learned the most from indulging in the creative process, and exploring my true identity.

And, what is the nature of my individuality? Love.

Yeah, even in the presence of absolute insanity, the witness continues witnessing, and the phenomenon of cosmic illusion keeps on coming, materializing and dematerializing constantly. In the presence of the great creator, the mover who is not moved.

Or, perhaps I'm mistaken. After all, I have indeed made some pretty big mistakes in the past. I mistook myself for the messiah. That's one of the biggest mistakes a man can make. And, yet, we are all 'the one'. Each and every one of us contains a spark of the divine light that permeates the entire known universe.

Now, knowing this, I can go forth in this lifetime freely. And, having shared my story with you, the reader, I can honestly say that I've lived and I've learned. Perhaps the most profound thing that I've learned is that I know nothing.

The weather outside is wintery. The skies are grey, and the air is wet and cold. On days like this one, I consider myself lucky to have a roof over my head, even if the guy upstairs is not a type-cast beacon of enlightenment, what with all his thumping and screaming. The ceiling of my apartment is the floor of his apartment. And, in my heart of hearts, I am reminded that he and I are in the same boat, so to speak. I forgive him for waking me up early this morning, shouting: *This is the last moment of your life!* After all, you can't argue with the truth.

His Tourettes-inspired philosophy is not flawed. It's actually perfectly simple. And, I know that, even when he is in the throws of mental illness, he is speaking to me. Just as it is his destiny to confront his inner demons, it is my destiny to learn from his suffering and forgive the wandering pilgrim who is suddenly found to be the teacher. We live, and we learn.

Even now, in the dark of winter, there is found a sense of hope. Yesterday, as a matter of fact, while I was walking along the seawall with my mother, we noticed the crocuses popping up out of the ground, and we also saw the first few cherry blossoms appearing on one of the trees.

My birthday is coming up. I will be thirty-seven. I remember my life as of yet, with all it's ups and downs. Hallucinations, at the age of five. Delusional anorexia, at the age of ten. A personality change, at the age of fourteen. Experimentation with marijuana, at the age of sixteen. Thinking I was from Mars, at the age of seventeen. Hypergraphia, in my late teens and early twenties. The Golden Dawn. The raves. The pregnancy. Diagnosis. Fatherhood. Denial, insight, acceptance, and then finally, a sense of self-embrace!

On the topic of recovery (or, 're-dis-covery', as the case may be), I am proud of how far I've come. I am giving back to the community at large, through peer support work and presentations. And, I hope this book has helped the reader to better and more fully understand the human element of mental illness.

On the topic of the future, I can honestly say that it is filled with hope. I hope that my father and my son both know that I love them greatly. The motto of BCSS is: *A reason to hope. The means to cope.* And, that pretty well sums it up. It has been an honour to volunteer my time and energy to educating people, over these past eight years. In fact, my next presentation is scheduled for my thirty-seventh birthday.

Now, in preparation for the upcoming talk at UBC, I plan to mention the aforementioned BCSS motto. My reason to hope is my son. He is going to need a happy and healthy father in his life. And, my means to cope, on a practical level, involves me carrying an extra dose of orally dissolving antipsychotic medication in my pocket. All I can say is: *Thank God for PRN's!* With or without the voices, my life will turn out fine.

LOOK WHAT THEY'VE DONE TO CATFISH HUNTER
CHAPTER 54

PERFECTION IS A FUNNY THING. I BELIEVE THAT THE ANSWER TO LIFE exists somewhere between being all and being nothing, between having all and having nothing, between thinking all and thinking nothing, between feeling all and feeling nothing, between willing all and willing nothing, between analyzing all and analyzing nothing, between balancing all and balancing nothing, between creating all and creating nothing, between perceiving all and perceiving nothing, between wielding all and wielding nothing, between knowing all and knowing nothing, and between believing all and believing nothing.

Like the mottos belonging to the twelve signs of the zodiac, the truth is found in the equilibrium of existence. My dad has always been an all-or-nothing kind of man. And, my mother has always been obsessed with perfection. My brother and I are just chips of the old block, in terms of our spiritual orientation.

A little bit of wisdom goes a long way. I've learned that it is foolish for me to believe in my delusional perceptions, and that it is wise to see things as they are. As a great philosopher has said: *a rose is a rose is a rose.*

Come to think of it, a daffodil is also a daffodil is also a daffodil.

Eternally, I am left to contemplate the meaning of my existence. If I'm not the messiah, who is? This is the question that I most often grapple with. On a daily basis, believe it or not. If it's not me, then I'd like to meet that man.

But, I am perfectly prepared to live the remainder of my life, pondering this concept. Back in 2001, I was wondering the very same thing. If I'm not the world saviour, then who is? Where does he live? What coffeeshop does he frequent? Does he dress in jeans and a teeshirt? How much money is in his bank account? What colour is his hair? Who are his parents? How old is he? And, perhaps most importantly, what is his name?

Old Catfish Hunter, a major league baseball pitcher from the 1970's, had a handlebar moustache, if memory serves me correctly. He was born, he lived, he died, and he was born again. A good way to illustrate the name-changing that I've gone through in my life is to say: *I was Bryn, I lived, I died, and I was Bryn again.*

DELETE

CHAPTER 55

A DAY DOES NOT GO BY WHERE I DON'T WISH I COULD HAVE DONE things differently. Maybe, some time in the not too distant future of this world, we will all be able to revise the rough draft of our mortal lives, honing it and honing it until it is perfect.

Now, there is a piece of hand-carved furniture on sale, at London Drugs, where I get my medication once a month. I've been eyeing it for the past few weeks or so. But, even though it has been reduced in price twice, it is still above and beyond my price range at the moment. It's a kind of box trunk on four legs, with a decorative lid and ornamental sides. I'm dying to know if my entire ten hardbound volume set of my written series 'Father Son' would fit inside the trunk. Later today, I will go there and measure it with a ruler.

Going to the pharmacy once a month, I am always amazed when they call my name over the loudspeaker to let me know that my prescription is ready. Usually, I'm busy trying to decide which brand of coffee bean to buy, or which toothpaste to get, or simply admiring the overpriced furniture.

Especially, I am amazed that the pharmacists who have been working there for years know my last name, even before I tell them it. They're probably quite familiar with me, seeing as I take nearly six times the average dosage of olanzapine and twice the therapeutic dosage of risperidone. They're like: *Oh, here comes that guy who really must be crazy.*

Live and let live, I say. They are entitled to their opinion. And, I am entitled to mine.

Silence of mind is far more profound than any deafening roar.

Of course, I usually buy the cheapest coffee, and I only dream of owning the furniture. But, I only ask that they leave me to freely indulge in my fantasy a little longer. All men are entitled to their dreams. They can't take that away from me. Dreaming is not a criminal act.

From this day forward, I will try to continue educating people. And, though my fifty-five book series is complete, I will continue to write creatively. Writing the wrongs of this world!

Tomorrow is a provincial holiday. Family Day, in fact. And, I will not be working. I will be spending the day with my son, as a matter of fact. We will probably have lunch together, at Granville Island. And, I will give him his new year's gift that I bought in chinatown. Then, in the evening, I will make sure that he gets on the ferry safely. He will return to his mom, who will be waiting for him on the Sunshine Coast. I am so very proud of both of them. They are so strong.

He demonstrates extraordinary skill and determination with the art of acting, and memorizes his lines impeccably. She takes good care of him, in terms of providing transportation, communication, food, shelter, clothing, and yes, you guessed it: *peace of mind.*

Early this morning, at about 7:30am, when I heard the guy upstairs shouting, I couldn't help but listen intently to just what he was trying to say. It's true, this *is* the last moment of my life. But, it is also the first moment of my life. You know me, with all of my delusions about the first and the last. But, I didn't cast judgment on the man. I only listened. And, in his words, as in the word of God, I detected a brilliant filament in the lightbulb of his convictions.

Sleep did not find me again. Nor did dream. I threw back the blankets of my bed, and reached for my cell phone, to see what time it was. I had been in bed for eleven hours, and felt thoroughly rested and rejuvenated. I went to the washroom, then went into the kitchen to make some breakfast. Listening to the radio, I sat there in the dining area of my living room, and realized that I didn't have any cream for my coffee. So, I went to the grocery store, and bought 500ml of Avalon half-and-half, along with a few organic bananas.

Under my breath, as I walked back along 7th avenue, I puffed on my cigarette.

Now, it is high noon, and I am back in my apartment, listening. Listening to the voice of my muse. Listening to the words of God. Listening to the guy upstairs.

Sometimes, I remember back to my life at Rainbow Lake. Back in those years, I was living the life of a solitary hermit of sorts, studying the Cabala, doing rituals, writing epic poetry. The water I drank was found in the freshwater creek, and the wood I burned to heat my house was found in the nearby grove.

To this very day, I also recall the magical process of discovering my monastic life within the order, along with all my brothers and sisters in the great work. One day, when I was a teenager, when my father and his wife had bought the ranch, we went up a small trail that led through the bush, along a four hour journey to the slopes above tree-line.

As soon as I got to the alpine tundra slopes of grass and glacier snow, I looked up from my feet, and turned around. The sight was enchanting. I could see all the way to the coastal mountain ranges. It was a clear blue sky. The vision of the immaculate landscape still haunts me to this very day.

Really, I am a typical Pisces. I'm nostalgic about nearly everything. Everything, except my hospitalizations, that is. There were mountains of suffering that even I could not climb. There were times of trial and trauma and timeless tribulation that even I was not prepared for. There were months and months of not knowing who I was. Then again, there were also days of peace.

EPILOGUE

BRIGHT BLUE SKIES, THIS MORNING, AS I LOOK OUT MY WINDOW. Yesterday was Chinese New Year, and the first time I'd seen my son in over a month. Around 2:00pm, my mother and I drove out to Burnaby to pick him up from his uncle's house. He looked exhausted, and we soon realized his fatigue was due to several days and nights of playing video games.

Ready to go, Gabriel stood there by the door, with his bags and things, munching on his toast and peanut butter. But, I had to ask if that was breakfast or lunch. Turns out it was breakfast, seeing as they had only just recently woken up.

Yeah, well... To be young again!

Now with toast in hand, Gabriel took the front seat, and I took the back seat. We drove east on Lougheed Highway, and soon arrived at my mother's house near Granville Island. We took about an hour just relaxing, having a *real* lunch, and then I gave my son his long-awaited gift. He opened the box, and saw the sword. He loved it. He thanked me. He gave me a big hug.

Gabriel, my mother and I went to Queen Elizabeth park for the afternoon, just before sunset. We drove to the top of the hill, parked, and explored the gardens. As the three of us walked around, under clear skies, I was experiencing mild symptoms. The quiet and subtle voices were prompting me to claim my world fame. But, all I wanted to do was enjoy a leisurely walk with my family, on Family Day. Was that too much to ask?

Eventually, we went inside the glass dome. There was a jungle contained therein, with several tropical parrots perching on trees and branches. It was nice to be warm, but there were too many people there.

Never had I seen Gabriel so very tired. But, we had fun. I think it was just that he needed food and sleep. So, just after sunset, we drove back to the house, and prepared dinner. While my mother was getting the hamburgers ready, my son and I walked over to Granville Island Public Market, in search of lettuce and tomatoes.

Early on in our hunt for organic produce, we realized that there was nothing of the sort. And, Gabriel refused to eat non-organic tomatoes, so we just got a head of Romaine lettuce to bring home.

Later on, we enjoyed a good dinner at the dining room table. And, then we watched a movie on the television. Soon, it was approaching my bedtime, which also implies that I had to take my meds soon. So, I bid them both a fond farewell, and walked back to my apartment.

Like clockwork, as soon as I entered my suite, I reached for pills and a tall glass of water. benztropine, risperidone and olanzapine (in that order). By the time 8:00pm rolled around, I was in bed, knowing that my son was probably on his way to the ferry terminal. Drowsy from the antipsychotic medications, I was asleep before I knew it.

Everything about yesterday's visit was good. But, life is bittersweet. I kinda wish my son hadn't spent quite so much time playing video games. And, I kinda wish we had found organic tomatoes. And, I kinda wish that I hadn't had to interrupt our visit by going home and taking my meds. But, there you have it. Life is bittersweet.

Did I worry about my thirteen year old son getting home alright? Yes. Is that normal for a father to do? Absolutely. I guess this was my first attempt at 'normal'. So, first thing this morning, I texted my mother to confirm that Gabriel had made it back to the Sunshine Coast okay. She replied, saying that this was indeed the case.

I guess life goes on. It always has, and it always will.

Tomorrow, I am going to meet with a psychiatrist whom I've never met before. I'm a bit nervous, but I'm actually looking forward to it. It's always good to get feedback from others, with regards to monitoring my mental health. I feel fine, but my case manager is worried about me, hence the visit with a new doctor.

My life has been filled with so many things. Innocence. Beauty. Tragedy. Courage. Determination. The list goes on. I've experienced a lot. But, perhaps the one most memorable moment was when I was about the same age as my son is now, climbing trails in the forest with my father. When I finally got above tree-line, I looked behind me. I was able to see forever.

And, perhaps the second most memorable moment was when I saw my infant son smile for the very first time. I could tell right away that he had a good sense of humour.

Reflecting on my life, these last couple months, I've explored my understanding of who I am. But, I've also learned that, between me and myself, there is a mountain. There are rolling foothills at the base, where alpine meadows and lakes pepper the landscape. There are thousands of evergreen trees all up and down the sides. Then, where the tree-line meets the tundra grasslands, and where the ground looks like something from another planet, complete with scattered red rocks and black Obsidian, I look to the peak. And, the further away you are from the peak the closer it seems, and the closer you get to the peak the further away it seems. There, eight thousand feet above sea level, the cinder cone left over from an old volcano lies erect, where black crags exclaim the essence of magnanimity. The rhythm of the wind. The fragrant smell of mortal freedom…

So, if you know nothing else, know that I'm gonna *climb* that mountain!

Finis.

CPSIA information can be obtained
at www.ICGtesting.com
Printed in the USA
LVOW13s1002261116

514539LV00013B/364/P